WITHDRAWN

SO-AIG-684

658
Sa7a

127904

DATE DUE			

The Androgynous Manager

The Androgynous Manager

Alice G. Sargent

Foreword by Elsa A. Porter

CARL A. RUDISILL LIBRARY
LENOIR RHYNE COLLEGE

amacom *A Division of American Management Associations*

658
Sa 7a
127904
ma. 1984

Excerpt from *The Velveteen Rabbit*, by Margery Williams (1958).
Reprinted by permission of Doubleday & Company, Inc.

"Did I Sound OK?" from Natasha Josefowitz, *Paths to Power:
A Woman's Guide from First Job to Top Executive* (Reading, Mass.:
Addison-Wesley, 1980). Reprinted by permission.

Library of Congress Cataloging in Publication Data

Sargent, Alice G., 1939–
   The androgynous manager.

   Includes bibliographical references and index.
   1. Management.   2. Androgyny (Psychology)
3. Sex role. I. Title.
HD38.S3143   658   80-69681
ISBN 0-8144-5568-9   AACR2

© 1981 AMACOM
A division of American Management Associations, New York.
All rights reserved.
Printed in the United States of America.

This publication may not be reproduced, stored in a retrieval
system, or transmitted in whole or in part, in any form or by
any means, electronic, mechanical, photocopying, recording,
or otherwise, without the prior written permission of
AMACOM, 135 West 50th Street. New York, N. Y. 10020.

Second Printing

*To my androgynous manager,
my daughter,
Elizabeth*

Foreword

"Unhappy are the people who haven't the words to describe what is going on," Thurman Arnold wrote almost half a century ago. For those who have been struggling to understand what is going on in American organizations today, *androgyny* is a happy word. It helps to describe part of a very complex, intense, inchoate effort under way to enable people to develop the best that is in them and to use their energies positively within their organizations and the society around them.

The responsibility for this effort rests mainly with the leaders and managers of our organizations. They run the machinery of society: business, government, education, philanthropy, politics, and so on—the panoply of interconnected parts that make up our social, political, and economic system. The system itself is suffering stress in all its parts. Not since the Great Depression, when Thurman Arnold wrote that line, has this country been so beset with problems for which it has no clear solutions. Inflation and unemployment appear intractable. Energy independence eludes us.

Pollution persists. The War on Poverty is not won. Government has not solved these problems, and now, in fact, is considered by the electorate to be a problem in itself—bloated and unresponsive. On the industrial front, our productivity is declining and with it the standard of living that has made us the envy of the globe. "We have rarely known a time when the nation seemed so conscious of its problems and so uncertain of its ability to respond with vigor and imagination," lamented Harvard University president Derek Bok in his 1980 annual report.

When all the complex issues are sorted out—the demographic changes affecting the society, the aspirations of women and minorities, the impact of technology, the reality of a global economy, and our universal dependence on diminishing quantities of fossil fuels—the need for vigorous and imaginative leadership becomes paramount. It is clearly the issue of the day. Where are the leaders and managers who can pull the society out of its present doldrums? What qualities and competencies must they have? How do these differ from the past?

Alice Sargent proposes a definition of leadership that draws on the best in all of us, both men and women. She calls it *androgynous*, having the characteristics of both sexes. But the key to her use of the term is balanced coexistence, as in the Chinese concept of *yin* and *yang*, male and female forces acting equally within nature to build and sustain the world around us. Effective leaders and managers need to use both logic and intuition, recognize both facts and feelings, be both technically competent and emotionally caring.

Until recently, the definition of managerial competence has excluded most feminine characteristics. The respected leader or manager was a highly competitive, power-driven person whose personal feelings were systematically submerged. The character of such contemporary leaders and managers was vividly described by Michael Maccoby in *The Gamesman* (Simon & Schuster, 1976). His message was that managerial leadership, deprived of compassion and caring, was destructive of the human values that undergird our society. He described a few exceptional leaders who combined compassion and idealism with their gamesman entrepreneurial qualities. They were "a kind of managerial mutant, a new corporate type, the gamesman who develops his heart as well as his head, and who could become an example for leadership in a changing society where the goal is economic democracy and the humanization of technology" (p. 244).

In this book, Alice Sargent adds the perspective of women and minorities, two groups who are new to their management roles and for whom the imitation of the old male model of leadership has been personally difficult and painful. We have to ask why that is so. Why don't women and many minority males fit the managerial roles now defined by most white males? Or if they do fit, if there are no real differences, then why this consternation about sex roles and the relative importance of being either a man or a woman in a position of leadership?

The answer is that sex does count. Cultural differences count. There *are* differences between the way men and women manage in most organizations. Sargent looks at these differences and their strengths and relative weaknesses. She concludes that neither, alone, provides an adequate model for management in this decade. The issue for women is not to imitate men. Rather, it is for women to adopt the best that men have to offer, and for men to do the same with the contributions that women bring.

The prescription is probably too easy. Such monumental social reconditioning is not easily accomplished. For in the last analysis it involves the complicated matter of ego and self-esteem. It brings into question the early social conditioning that establishes the boundaries within which self-esteem is gained and preserved. For most men, self-esteem is integrally connected to winning competitions, either as individuals or as part of a team. To be male is to be a warrior. The social expectations of warriors are that they will always be strong and courageous. They never cry. They fight to win. Warriors have territories that they are expected to protect. Any incursion into their turf is perceived as a threat to their power and their ego.

In our modern world, these battles are fought daily in the

bureaucracies of public agencies and private corporations. Most women working in these organizations are amazed at the issues that . become grounds for battle: the size or placement of an office, the number of people on a staff, the order of precedence in a hierarchy, the elegance of a title. Often the *appearance* of power becomes the reality for which many men seem to strive. They get caught in organizational conflicts, large and small, where the issue of the common good is more often than not submerged in the petty struggle of egos. No one will yield or admit he is wrong, for to do so diminishes his masculine self-esteem. In an article in *Esquire* magazine (May 1980), Barbara Tuchman questions why, in the course of human history, man has governed so unwisely. She draws this conclusion:

> Males, who so far in history have managed government, are obsessed with potency, which is the reason, I suspect, why it is difficult for them to admit error. I have rarely known a man who, with a smile and a shrug, could easily acknowledge being wrong. Why not? *I* can; without any damage to self-respect. I can only suppose the difference is that deep in their psyches, men somehow equate being wrong with being impotent.

Women are not put to that test. But they, too, hold limiting self-concepts. Feelings of dependency and powerlessness, as imaginary but as psychically real as notions of masculine impotence, can paralyze otherwise competent women. Assertiveness training may help some women, but the real antidote has to be a personally deepened self-trust and self-esteem. That comes only by experiencing achievement in one's job, as many of Sargent's women so poignantly attest.

Each sex has its own dragons to slay. That they can help one another is clearly the good news this book conveys. Our age could well mark the beginning of the end of the War Between the Sexes! However, we cannot underestimate the power that the dominant male mentality has had and continues to have in our lives. To struggle against that norm is no easy task. The very litigiousness of our society can be described as a manifestation of maleness. This point was made especially vivid to me by Carol Gilligan's report of her study of young girls growing up. Watching the girls at play, Gilligan noticed that when there was a conflict, they stopped the game and did not proceed until the relationships were mended. If the conflict was too deep, the game was abandoned. Girls, she concluded, were more concerned about maintaining the relationships they had with one another than about playing the game. Boys, on the other hand, were more concerned about winning or losing. Their way of managing conflict was to have rules. If someone broke a rule, the game would be stopped, an appropriate judgment would be rendered, and the game would then continue. They respected the rules more than they did their relationships. In fact, boys who disliked one another could play effectively on the same team, since their aim was not necessarily friendship, but winning.

Rules certainly have their place in society. Consider for a moment what chaos would ensue if we abandoned all rules and adjudicated every conflict in the context of the existing situation! That would be the extreme of "feminine" behavior as Carol Gilligan describes it. But consider as well the vast proliferation of rule making in our society, and the consequent litigiousness (and the burgeoning number of lawyers, including, of course, women). Have we not reached an excess of rule making? Are we not experiencing runaway *yang*, or maleness, in our culture, relying solely on rule making and regulation to govern conflicts that might better be resolved by examining the underlying relationships of one part of the society to the other?

A rule-bound society can produce order. But carried to extremes it produces bloody adversaries. And that, it seems, is where we are today. Business perceives government as an enemy, concocting injurious rules. Government assumes that business and industry will evade the rules. The rules, themselves, ought to concern the common good. They are pushed into place by people who care deeply about the quality of life on this planet—about clean air, clean water, the health and safety of workers, and the end of oppression for classes of our society. But in struggling to achieve each particular "right," these special-interest groups lose sight of the needs of the whole society. Business cannot be the enemy of government, or vice versa. The two must be partners in developing the commerce among people without which our standards of living cannot be sustained. People who care about the environment also need to care about the needs of the people for whom the environment provides basic sustenance. Balances need to be struck so that harmony can be maintained among our separate needs and interests.

The movement toward androgyny in management is part of the larger movement toward balance in the society at large. It cannot come too soon! Jean Houston tells us that in times of chaos, like our own, the rise of the feminine principle is a sign of hope. It promises to redress the imbalance between compassion and conflict that marks our present organizational lives. Let us hope so, but let us also not leave it to chance.

Each and every manager, male and female, can contribute to the process of civilization by learning how to become androgynous. Androgyny means unlearning our negative behaviors and learning how to become equally contributing human beings. In the last analysis, it means growing up, shedding the excesses of both male and female adolescence that in the past have limited our human experience. It means becoming fully human.

Elsa A. Porter
Former Assistant Secretary for Administration
U. S. Department of Commerce

Acknowledgments

The Androgynous Manager has been germinating for the past five years. I am grateful to the organizations that lent support to the idea of androgyny by asking me to speak at professional meetings and thereby gave dignity to the notion:

Aerospace Corporation
American Society for Public Administration
American Society for Training and Development
Federal Executive Institute
    Allen Hard, Ph.D., and Robert Matson, Ph.D.
National Training Laboratories Institute
Organization Development Network
Organization Development Practitioner Magazine
    Larry Porter, Editor
Overseas Private Investment Corporation
University Associates
U.S. Department of Commerce
    Elsa Porter and Lynden V. Emerson

I am also grateful to many colleagues who devoted their energy to filling out the cumbersome questionnaires that yielded such helpful vignettes and data for this book.

My respect and appreciation go to Katherine Janka of Park City, Utah, and to Ian McNett of Madison, Virginia, for their extremely helpful editorial assistance and overall response to the book. In addition, I am very grateful to Leonard Goodstein, president of University Associates, for his thoughtful and constructive reading of the manuscript. Susan Olin of Washington, D.C., helped maintain remarkable order over the numerous references and correspondence.

This book was typed from start to finish in all its various drafts by Joan Corwin of San Diego, California. Joan's ability to hold things together, to persevere, and to make sense of my word-smithing is a testimony to her own excellent androgynous skills. She has brought warmth, humor, and competence to our association.

My ongoing highly valued relationship with Jim Thickstun, M.D., of La Jolla continues to contribute to my own androgynous behavior. I am also grateful for the assistance of Buford Macklin of Washington, D.C., a committed line manager, who is part of my support system. He served as a reality check for many of the ideas in this book. As always, my colleagueship and friendship with Melinda Sprague Mackenzie of Princeton, New Jersey, helps provide balance in my work and life.

Alice G. Sargent

Contents

What Is Real?

"What is Real?" asked the Rabbit one day, when they were lying side by side near the nursery fender, before Nana came to tidy the room. "Does it mean having things that buzz inside you and a stick-out handle?"

"Real isn't how you are made," said the Skin Horse. "It's a thing that happens to you. When a child loves you for a long, long time, not just to play with, but *really* loves you, then you become Real."

"Does it hurt?" asked the Rabbit.

"Sometimes," said the Skin Horse, for he was always truthful. "When you are Real you don't mind being hurt."

"Does it happen all at once, like being wound up," he asked, "or bit by bit?"

"It doesn't happen all at once," said the Skin Horse. "You become. It takes a long time. That's why it doesn't often happen to people who break easily, or have sharp edges, or who have to be carefully kept. Generally, by the time you are Real, most of your hair has been loved off, and your eyes drop out and you get loose in the joints and very shabby. But these things don't matter at all, because once you are Real you can't be ugly, except to people who don't understand."

Margery Williams
The Velveteen Rabbit

Prologue

As women, Blacks, Hispanics, Asians, and American Indians began to move into the world of management, the emphasis was not on learning from them. Efforts focused, instead, on fitting minorities and women into what once was the domain of white men. These efforts almost totally missed the point by failing to take advantage of the new resources being brought to the management world. Interestingly, though, as affirmative action has gained ground, management theory and practice are expanding the concept of what makes a good manager. The new members of the workforce exhibit many of the behaviors that are being discussed and very tentatively tried out by managers.

As concern for people inches toward parity with concern for getting the job done, managers will have to exercise greater skills in dealing with people. They will need to express and accept emotions, nurture and support colleagues and subordinates, and promote interactions between bosses and subordinates and between leaders and members of work teams. These behaviors are desirable not only

1

for their own sake, but because they can increase organizational effectiveness and efficiency. Since many of these behaviors traditionally have been regarded as "feminine," and therefore not acceptable in the marketplace, both male and female managers have avoided them. Instead managers have been expected to be aggressive, rational, autonomous, task-oriented, and tough-minded.

The new management style does not call for abandoning traditional "masculine" behaviors but for blending them with "feminine" behaviors. As we shall see, the demands of the workplace increasingly require this balance. In addition, the greater number of options promise a richer, fuller life at work and at home for both men and women. In order to be effective and healthy, all of us need a mix of both masculinity and feminity.

The word *androgyny* describes this new management mode. As a psychological term, androgyny suggests that it is possible for people to exhibit both masculine and feminine qualities and that such values, attitudes, and behaviors reside in varying degrees in each of us. The thesis of this book is that an androgynous mix of behaviors is the most effective management style in the workplace in the 1980s—a style that blends behaviors previously deemed to belong exclusively to men or women.

What is equally significant, if not more so, is that androgyny is also the best route to fulfillment in our personal lives. It holds out the possibility that we might feel human and whole in both the workplace and the home—that we might express autonomy and interdependence in all our relationships and feel like balanced emotional and rational people wherever we go. Certain aspects of intimate relationships are becoming relevant to organizational life. Both at home and at work we need a supportive culture that includes the opportunity to have intellectual and emotional rapport with those around us; the chance to be vulnerable and to take risks in order to learn; and the chance to utilize a problem-solving approach rather than a blaming one.

Andro is the Greek root for male and *gyne* is the Greek root for female. The poet Samuel Taylor Coleridge used the word *androgynous* to describe the qualities of mind in which a poetic spirit is coupled with a logical approach. He said, "The truth is, a great mind must be androgynous, having the characteristics of both sexes." Virginia Woolf described her personal struggle within the same framework in *A Room of One's Own*. She wrote:

> It is fatal to be a man or woman pure and simple; one must be woman-manly or man-womanly. Some collaboration has to take place between the woman and the man before the act of creation can be accomplished. The whole of the mind must be wide open if we are to get the sense that the writer is communicating experience with perfect fullness. There must be freedom and there must be peace.[1]

Traditional sex roles have created a sharp division of labor around sex-linked behavior for both men and women. As characterized by sociologist Talcott Parsons, masculinity has been associated with an instrumental or problem-solving approach and femininity with an expressive approach that involves a concern for others' welfare and for group cohesiveness. David Bakan, a psychologist, has used the terms "agentic orientation" (a concern for oneself as an individual) for masculinity and "communal orientation" (a concern for one's relationship to others) for femininity.

Masculinity and femininity may become negative and even destructive when they are represented in extreme and unadulterated form. This point is made clear by psychologist Sandra Bem, who developed the Androgyny Scale (see Appendix A) and has been instrumental in fostering the concept of psychological androgyny: "Extreme femininity, untempered by sufficient concern for one's own needs as an individual, may produce dependency and self-denial, just as extreme masculinity, untempered by a sufficient concern for the needs of others, may produce arrogance and exploitation."[2] What I am suggesting throughout this book is an integration rather than a polarization of the characteristics of toughness and tenderness, of connectedness and autonomy. Then a manager may combine being a tough battler, friendly helper, and logical thinker.

An increasing body of literature and experience suggests that androgyny in management makes not only for happier people but also for better managers. My own experience began in affirmative action work in the mid-1970s with a large manufacturing corporation. I was involved in an effort to move women into nontraditional, mostly management positions. It was like turning warm, spontaneous people into mechanical figures whose behavior was almost exclusively determined by their work roles. I watched as attractive, compassionate, and vital women were hired into an all-male, highly rational, problem-solving environment. In effect what the organization was semiconsciously doing was encouraging the women to act like men. Although they didn't want to lose their identities, these women also feared they wouldn't make it if they didn't adapt their behavior. They considered themselves defenseless against endless, albeit frequently well-meaning, feedback that served only to underline how inadequate and out of place they felt.

One woman said, "I was afraid, afraid of buying in, like the minute I gave in I would become one of them. I'd become competitive, screw-your-buddies tough, and so concerned about the job I wouldn't care about my family."

Men have been paying the price for toughness all along. One male line manager commented:

I do see the costs of being male, of not being a person really. If people expect you to be the strong one, always reliable, financially responsible, emotionally restrained, not expressing extremes of joy or sorrow, not able to show fatigue, not able to have down time, all things associated with dependency, that's a big burden. Not being androgynous, you can run a hierarchical ship. People will follow your directives. But with a concern for people, there's a lot more support; you can handle crises much more easily. The ramifications of caring are great. It adds flavor; things are richer.

This line manager recognized not only the problems of the old style of management but also the rewards of allowing one's "feminine" side to surface at work.

Today, many men are balking at the old ways, particularly at the possibility of shaving ten years off their lives from the stress associated with the masculine style of management or at uprooting their families in order to move around the country to comply with capricious company policy. New attitudes about adult development have led us all to focus on our continued growth. We have acquired a sense that to be effective today we have to behave differently. As one vice-president of manufacturing said, "We have gone about as far as we can go in increasing productivity by leaning on technology. The only way we can significantly increase production is to be concerned about people."

You may now be saying, "This is nothing more than human resources management—something we've been talking about for ten years. It's just packaged another way." Yes and definitely no.

Adopting a concept of management that incorporates both masculine and feminine behaviors is a significant and controversial next step in freeing all people to behave in ways that can benefit them both personally and professionally. In the past these behaviors have been disallowed to them because they belonged to one sex or the other. It has been more costly for men to express feminine behavior than for women to express masculine behavior. Generally, however, women express masculine behavior primarily in the marketplace. At home or on social occasions, many women have found it necessary to revert to the feminine posture. Men have found it more or less legitimate to express feminine behavior at home, but *not* in the marketplace.

Participants in management development programs express a desire to change their behavior. Men arrive and say, "I've been told I have to learn to be more sensitive." Women in these programs want to learn to deal with power and conflict, to be assertive, and to stop personalizing feelings. In essence, our culture has expected one thing of men and another of women. Men have been socialized to exhibit autonomy and women to show dependence. Now it appears that women are trying to learn about autonomy and men are trying to learn about intimacy.

Organizational reward systems that support these new behaviors are slowly emerging. For example, the performance appraisal system in one government organization includes an evaluation of both interpersonal competence and team effectiveness. Not only had these behaviors previously not been actively rewarded, but there wasn't even widespread agreement that they were crucial to managerial effectiveness.

It seems necessary that men practice being nurturant and spontaneous and allow themselves to experience feelings, and that organizations value these qualities, in order for women to be able to hold on to these seemingly second-class "feminine" qualities. The organization could become a multicultural environment where people learn behaviors, attitudes, and values from each other rather than where one sex does all the teaching and the other all the learning, to the detriment of everyone.

You may be saying, "We want to live in a sex-role-free society. Doesn't androgyny encourage sex-role stereotyping? We want behavior to have no gender." There is an irony here. As Sandra Bem says:

> The concept of androgyny contains an inner contradiction and, hence, the seeds of its own destruction. . . . Androgyny necessarily presupposes that the concepts of masculinity and femininity themselves have distinct and substantive content. But to the extent that the androgynous message is absorbed by the culture, the concepts of masculinity and femininity will cease to have such content and the distinctions to which they refer will blur into invisibility. Thus, when androgyny becomes a reality, the concept of androgyny will have been transcended.[3]

We are not at that point in our culture in the 1980s. We may not reach that point in our lifetimes. As sociologist Philip Slater said in a recent speech, "The women's movement is the most important liberation movement in history. All other social upheavals in history usually have ended, even after considerable progress, with a patriarchal hierarchy; but this one gradually is forcing both sexes into a more holistic perspective on the world."

This book is an attempt to delineate a model of androgynous behavior. The model is not intended to be normative or ideal, but rather to increase the options for all of us. It presents a smorgasbord of ideas, offering the range of behaviors useful to being a whole person. A move toward androgynous behaviors may, in the short run, increase the inner turmoil for a boss or subordinate, a wife or husband. But in the long run such behaviors are critical to being effective in organizations, content in family life, and successful in achieving self-expression and meaningful contact with others.

An androgynous organization is one that strives to develop its people at the same time that it increases its productivity, and not to do either activity to the exclusion of the other. An androgynous person is one who strives to attain a balance in all relationships—at work, at home, and in the community; while playing racquetball, loving other people, starting a new project, having fun with kids, or taking long walks on the beach. Achieving this balance is a significant next step in moving us beyond our sex roles. It seems quite a lot to aspire to in one lifetime.

NOTES

1. Virginia Woolf, *A Room of One's Own* (New York: Harcourt, Brace & World, 1929), pp. 100–101.
2. Sandra Bem, "Androgyny and Mental Health." Paper presented at The American Psychological Association meeting, Chicago, 1975.
3. *Ibid.*

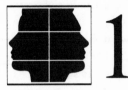

The Age of
Androgyny

While the age of androgyny is not here—nor is it likely to be here by the end of this century—an awareness is growing that the assignment of sex-role behaviors for men and women will never be the same again.

The energy, the purposefulness, the impetus for change, have existed for women throughout the past decade. While the actual numbers grow slowly, the vision is there. Nonetheless, women around the world are still overworked, underpaid, poorly educated in technical fields, and lacking the political and economic power to effect rapid change. However, in urban areas particularly, women are trickling into management, as evidenced by the numerous new magazines for women—*Savvy, New Women*, and *Working Women*. These new careerwomen pushing their way at least to the middle and some to the top of the management heap are buying into the same myths and suffering the accompanying price of stress and single-mindedness that the competitive style has cost men for decades.

9

At the same time, there are pockets of change among men in various parts of the country: men's centers, men's consciousness-raising groups, men for ERA, men championing custody rights, and men opposed to the draft. But in the marketplace, interest in and awareness of what it means to be a man, what costs society has exacted in return for conferring manhood, what's really in the women's movement that benefits men—all this comes slowly.

A manifestation of this lack of awareness came from a prominent male manager who recently said, "I can think of nothing more boring than to sit around and talk about what it means to be a man." He doesn't yet have any notion of the energy that will be released when he starts to unravel his sex-role expectations from his own inner view of himself as a person. He has not yet turned on to the plusses of relating to women as both competent and compassionate, of developing close friendships with men without constant fear of being labeled homosexual, and of reexamining his values to see what really matters to him. Instead, he continues to hunker down, shoulder to the grindstone, trudging on. None of this is his fault at all. He is simply responding to the experiences of his life. There's so much ahead for this sleeping prince, but he may not wake up in his lifetime.

Would that we could eclipse the developmental stages in the change process and gracefully slide into androgynous behavior—into greater options of social expression for both men and women. But such is not the way of change. It seems we move one lockstep at a time in the dialectical process. The next step in the 1980s is women becoming more like men, while men bemoan the fact that women are not like they used to be. Men say, "Women are getting so tough," and women decry the fact that there aren't any growth-oriented, independent men out there. In general, the caricature of women in organizations is that they are suppressing their tears, trying to think logically, dressing for success in black suits that suggest power, saying to men who call to ask them out for a drink, "I really need some alone time tonight," and generally becoming less tender people.

The caricature of men in organizations is that they are still highly task-oriented; they resist changes around them by complaining that what is going on is reverse prejudice or by saying we are going too fast. In addition, they most understandably feel victimized because they are hassled not only at work but also at home. Their wives may be going back to work or back to school, so they have to cook dinner and help out at home as well as train a new woman manager at the office.

It would be great to move quickly to the next stage rather than to inch our way agonizingly through this one. But the revolution is vast, and it takes·time to ripple out across the United States as well as internationally. It is easy to see how the process creeps slowly if we simply take a concept like networking among women. Through informal communications systems, or networks, women have begun to exchange contacts, information, and support, and thereby feel less isolated and alone. In Washington and New York networks are a highly organized phenomenon, but they are being discussed now only for the first time in Idaho Falls, and in Toronto. In many places, the term still needs a definition!

In some parts of the country, if two or more women are seen having coffee together, someone still will walk by to comment, "What are you plotting—a revolution?" If two minority people are seen together, usually the thought is not uttered. The phenomenon has not yet become natural and familiar, as it is among white men.

Another clear indication of how far we have to go is the controversy surrounding having working parents bring their children into the workplace when necessary. This issue still elicits powerful negative reactions. It is not yet considered natural to regard people at work as whole, as possessing a variety of roles, including a parent role, which may sometimes overlap or be in conflict with their work role. True, now 11 federal agencies have child-care centers in Washington and certain major corporations are setting up day-care opportunities at the workplace. But it is not the norm for parents at some point to take their children to work to show them what they do, let them see where they live eight to ten hours each day, or just be with them.

Traveling on short notice and traveling frequently are still considered loyalty tests in many organizations. Staying home with a child and not wanting to travel are seen to conflict with commitment to the business. Certainly there are business emergencies that require travel on short notice, and a commitment to the organization is necessary; but so too is it necessary for the organization to be concerned with issues of family life as well.

Organizations are slowly beginning to reevaluate the way they do business. They are groping for alternatives to regular business trips—such as periodic meetings where everyone is brought together and teleconferencing (utilized by the U.S. Department of Housing and Urban Development and by such corporations as the Atlantic Richfield Company in Los Angeles). In addition, the Ford Foundation allows its employees to accumulate credits for assistance from the organization to take spouses and children on trips.

But these are notions for the future, for the era when organizations do not ask people to shoulder by themselves the conflict between being a person and being a worker. Let us back up. This book is quite present-oriented. It will survey the landscape to see what the status quo is—what the trends are in management in the 1980s. It concludes that at least in the workplace certain behaviors are now being encouraged that support a vision of androgyny.

In *American Dreams: Lost and Found*, Studs Terkel explores the myth of success. The old dreams he describes, such as owning a piece of land and running a small-town paper, are now part of the aspirations of women as well as men. As Terkel says of the people who bespeak their dreams, "They may be catching. Unfortunately, it is not the kind of thing that is on the six o'clock news." Nonetheless, people do have a capacity for change. As Terkel notes, "There is human possibility. That's where all the excitement is. If you can be part of that, you're aware and alive. It's not a dream; it's possible. It's everyday stuff." Such is the dream of androgyny. As men and women tilt slightly toward each other's behaviors, we have the quiet murmurings of new ways of acting.

At the heart of the argument for androgyny is the recognition that within the next quarter of a century our competitive style of doing business will come under serious challenge. We are moving into an era of uncertainty. Keynesian economics is being called into question. The crises in energy and transportation continue. Every major field of knowledge is changing. Medical costs are higher than ever. Even worse, it seems a case of more not being any better: just spending money doesn't yield a solution.

These complex problems call for new approaches based on collaboration and interdependence rather than on competition. The solutions require risk and experimentation and working out problems together. They require a partnership among business, labor, and government so that the parts of the system do not stalemate one another.

The concept of androgyny—with its focus on interdependence and mutual support—holds out the promise that these challenges can be met. Androgyny heralds a new era for organizations and for workers in both their professional and personal lives. The spirit of this era is a concern for people not at the expense of productivity; and a concern for significant changes in interpersonal relationships between men and women in all sorts of configurations, as bosses and subordinates, and as peers.

One agency began a training program called "Starting Over" for its managers because it felt the issues surrounding the new work-force were so fresh that they heralded a new beginning. We are the pioneers unearthing the problems and cautiously searching out a few solutions for a phenomenon that in some future era will be common-place. For some of us, these efforts support a total vision of androgyny; for others, they are still random events. It really does not matter what we call our journey as long as we are out there scanning the map together.

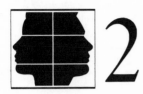

2

Building Androgynous Relationships in Organizations

The life of the women and minorities entering organizations today is not easy. Perhaps the greatest difficulty is that there is no end in sight, no new land ahead—just the opportunity to keep trudging on to be joined by other pioneers. The roles of women, minorities, and white males in the workforce are shifting. At first, the pattern was to try to mainstream the minorities and women who were entering the work environment for the first time. As they trickled into organizations, the clear message they got was to adopt the role that had been prescribed for white males. But more recently, as white males have begun to question the problems of mobility, stress, and workaholism, and as differences in the new workforce keep surfacing, there has been a slight breakthrough in the crust of organizations. It now appears that a few organizations are focusing on differences as well. Yet no one knows how much change will be necessary either in individuals or organizations. The answer probably is more change on each side than either wants.

The emergence of women in management and the social forces that foster androgyny raise several key issues that may produce barriers in male-female, boss-subordinate, and peer relationships in organizations. These include:

The need for support systems.
Control and power.
Dealing with emotions.
Dependency.
Dealing nondestructively with sexuality in organizations (a topic that will be dealt with at length in a later chapter).

What a far cry from traditional concerns of planning, staffing, organizing, delegating, analyzing, and evaluating! Yet they too focus on how people work together effectively to fulfill organizational goals and to meet human needs. And these issues, which have largely been ignored in the development of management theory and practice, raise critical questions about the functions of management:

- How do people who have been brought up to compete with each other learn to support each other?
- How do managers evaluate women employees when their style, though not the dominant organizational style, is effective in accomplishing organizational objectives?
- How do managers deal with conflict between organizational and family needs?
- How do men change their style when it conforms to organizational norms but causes stress for them?
- How do men express feelings at work?
- What does a manager do when faced with a man or woman crying or with an angry employee?
- How do people in organizations deal with sexual attraction in nonthreatening ways?
- How can managers make organizational life more creative and alive?

These issues relate to characteristics that are deeply embedded in the behaviors of one sex but foreign to the other. Men often don't

know they are acting "masculine," nor do women always know that
their behavior is "feminine." The behavior seems natural because it
has become so ingrained. Many don't stop to think about it, question
if it must always be so, or realize how freeing it might be to have
more options. Some organizations, in fact, oppose the acknowledg-
ment of differences, preferring to say that they treat everyone the
same. Issues like the ones enumerated above illustrate the complex-
ity of the problems confronting organizations as the composition of
the workforce shifts and as male values evolve in new directions.
The changes represent a challenging opportunity for managers to
develop a style that could increase both employee and organizational
effectiveness.

In preparation for this book, I conducted a survey of 50 line
managers to hear their assessment of the issues facing men and
women in organizations. What I found was that the line managers
were aware that there were problems and tensions but had difficulty
conceptualizing them. They still did not understand what some of
the static between men and women was all about. That fact added
urgency and energy to my desire to do this book. To collect more
data, I then went to 50 consultant colleagues in a variety of
organizations to hear their viewpoints. I asked questions about
female-male interactions in the workplace and sought ideas and
opinions as well as actual case studies. This chapter summarizes the
key issues, which will be discussed in greater depth throughout the
book.

Support: Whom Can I Turn To?

The corporate and the bureaucratic environments are lonely and
call out for support, especially during times of change. Today, the
powerful change in management styles and expectations is creating
discomfort and fear among the women and men who are sometimes
the victims, sometimes the agents of change. Women, faced with the
choice of adopting an alien style in order to advance or holding to an
unacceptable one and risking stagnation, need help from their
friends. Building an environment in which women can become

managers without ceasing to be women requires networks among
women and behavior change by men. Support also is needed by
Blacks, Hispanics, and other minorities who have stepped onto and
are seeking to climb the corporate ladder.

In my survey, women often spoke of the need for healthy support
from their male management peers and supervisors. Unfortunately,
such a need is often identified with so-called feminine dependency.
For these women, support meant being given the encouragement to
develop and use their skills, not finding someone to lean on. One
woman spoke of a "very supportive male boss who encouraged my
career development and cajoled me to assume responsibilities."
Margaret James-Neill, a consultant, said her "supportive" supervisor
was a man who "allowed me time and space but gave me clear
opportunities and had high expectations that demanded of me a firm
contribution to the work of the unit and the organization. He was
not competitive; was supportive; and pushed me to higher achievement, a behavior I have not always trusted in men." Others said
their most supportive relationships were with other women.

Support issues were important to Carol Gibson,* department
head at a large manufacturing organization. Hired after graduation
from college in an entry-management position, she said:

> My early expectations were very naive. I didn't know what I
> would be getting into working with men. I hadn't worked
> with a lot of men. It was painful. I didn't get support from
> my one woman co-worker. Not only did that not go well, but
> there wasn't support from any of the men. They didn't know
> how to help.

Gibson wanted support for her competence, support to help her
integrate herself into the organization and grow. A colleague, Ellen
Howe,* needed support to keep going as one of the first women

*Carol Gibson and Ellen Howe are extremely successful managers in a large
manufacturing corporation. Quotations from my interviews with them appear
throughout the book. What is important to note here is that they chose to use
pseudonyms because they did not feel it was yet timely to deal with their colleagues
about these issues.

managers in a warehouse assignment in the same organization. She said:

> Whom do you talk to, to say out loud, "I feel like I'm not going to make it"? I was plagued by self-doubt and discounts, and endless feedback. They said I didn't have the mentality of a manufacturing manager; I'm not tough enough, I'm too sensitive. I'd take things too personally from technicians. I would worry constantly about what I did wrong. I was open and vulnerable to criticism, and people who wanted to could easily upset me. I told people those things that were frustrating to me. I was basic and honest, and by being so, I told people how to get to me. I really opened myself up, and then I got hurt and closed myself down.

These two women needed a support network. It helps to know you're not the only one who is scared, self-doubting, struggling with new expectations and new behaviors. They needed people to talk to, people who would understand their confusion, pain, and anger. Such support mechanisms could be built into the organizational structure. The organization could anticipate the isolation, loneliness, and bewilderment and respond by establishing groups where men and women could share their experiences and their strategies.

Men rarely have the opportunity to share their feelings with other men. Generally, men have been socialized to deny that these needs exist. There are well-established information networks, business lunches, golf and racquetball clubs, and other ties for men that women and minorities find hard to penetrate. But men do lack support for shifting away from the dominant organizational style, especially in areas where they most certainly will feel unfamiliar and uncomfortable at first. There are few structures for men that support being sensitive, expressing feelings, being vulnerable and needy, or comforting others.

What are the thoughts and feelings of a 40-year-old male executive who is beginning to feel the pinch of his socialization? He may be at the peak of his career, or perhaps facing the lack of fit between his dreams and his reality. He may be in a 15- or 20-year marriage in which he has made trade-offs between intimacy and having a partner for life's tasks. Or he may be in a second marriage that holds out hopes for another chance at closeness. Somewhere he may have adolescent children who demand a great deal. He has lived his life with a strong goal-directed orientation, a heavy workaholic style. He has spent little time on introspection, on being tuned in to his inner feelings. Most of his relationships with men have focused on activities. Other men have served as a support system in the sense of companionship, but not for sharing feelings of loneliness, disappointment, or failure.

He has spent most of his life living up to the pressures of being a man. He has devoted his energy to satisfying work and family demands and perhaps has given up his own development in the process. Now he is restless and starting to open some of the closed doors.

Allen Hard, a faculty member at the Federal Executive Institute in Charlottesville, Virginia, describes some of the questions that arise in the minds of executives as they enter the midlife decade:

1. How important am I?

2. How far am I willing to compete? How much am I willing to continue to give up for the sake of my work?

3. What is it like to give up the dream of getting to the top?

4. How much intimacy do I have in my private life? Have I taken too much time away from home for my career?

5. My health is a concern to me. I operate under a lot of stress. I know people who have had heart attacks. I don't seem to be able to do things the way I did them before. I can't work as long without feeling the costs. I want to take charge of my life. I want to feel more in control.

6. I've always worked ten to twelve hours a day. Now, with car pools, there is a dramatic change in my life. I go home at five o'clock. Sometimes I resent it; sometimes I really like it. It has broken a pattern of many years. I need to build new activities at home.

7. The younger managers in the organization seem to talk

through decisions with their people. I don't think we're going to be seeing as much unilateral decision making anymore. I feel out of step.

8. I feel like I'm a role model all the time. Because I'm the boss I have to be aloof, demanding, prodding, not showing favoritism. I feel I can't relate to others as a real person or become friends with anyone who works with me.

9. I'm sick of moving around the country. I have the people I jog with at work and a group I eat lunch with on Fridays. My kids are in high school; my wife is completing her degree. The company can offer me all the moves it wants, but I'm not going to take them. I'm not going to face that kind of loneliness anymore.

For such an executive, support from peers, family, and friends is particularly important. Support structures need to be established to help men uncover and share their feelings and renew their own development. Major change is unlikely to come about if men remain isolated in making these shifts.

Competence: How Do You Know She's Competent?

The competent woman may not look like the competent man. How do you tell? Men have been socialized to value having an impact, to express primarily task-oriented or instrumental behavior. Women, on the other hand, have been praised for expressiveness and vicarious accomplishments; their identity is strengthened through the development of others. However, the groundrules of organizational culture are that power, charisma, and effectiveness are to some degree demonstrated through action—through giving advice, influencing others, having presence, and having the reputation that comes with doing all these things. This requires a different kind of visibility from the one that many women have. For example, studies show that in a group discussion men speak two-thirds of the time and women one-third.

Since many women expect a high level of expertise from themselves, they try not speak up unless they're sure of the facts.

They overemphasize the power of knowledge and underemphasize the power of their position. They know that because they are so visible, mistakes are all the more costly. Frequently, they also express their feelings before stating their opinions or solutions, and so appear pokey to respond. A male manager trying to coach a new female manager said, "You're just not thinking fast enough, or putting your ideas out quickly enough for our culture here. By the time you get part way through what you're saying people will be thinking of what else they have to do, drumming on their pads with pencils, or staring out the window." What he reported was absolutely true. What he failed to do was to question an organizational style that fostered competition and responding to crises and failed to value introspection and feelings. So the competent woman may not appear as capable of responding rapidly to new ideas or even working to have an impact. Yet her style can offer the organization valuable benefits in certain situations—particularly in fostering collaboration and teamwork in groups. This is not to say that she does not need to become more systematic and logical, to draw her ideas together into a model, to deal with conflict, to depersonalize situations, and to be more direct.

Eileen Morley, a consultant in Cambridge, Massachusetts, and previously a faculty member at the Harvard Business School, described men's style as "think-feel" and women's style as "feel-think."[1] Asked what he's feeling, a man may report what he's thinking. Asked what she is thinking, a woman may report what she's feeling. Women often express their feelings at what appear to others as inappropriate moments. Therefore, they don't seem to be rational, analytic thinkers—the mode with which organizations and men are most comfortable. Many women need to assert their analytical abilities and use persuasive arguments more frequently, while many men need to examine their overuse of the rational, logical, analytical, problem-solving style.

For some men, the fact that a manager is a woman is prima facie evidence of lack of competence. Gibson described her experience:

When I went out to work on the production floor as a team manager, it was a period of great struggle. I was trying to take care of 22 people's needs as well as my own. I had my technicians doubting me! The team managers discounted me by not taking my word for how the shift went, and they complained about how I left at the end of my shift. They would gang up to resolve the mechanical problem but wouldn't ask me for technical advice. Instead, they went directly to my technicians for advice.

Even after she had grown in her job and learned the machinery, Gibson found that men left her out of technical discussions.

By the time of my second performance appraisal, I got the feedback that I had grown technically. Still, I wasn't included in technical conversations with the other managers. They conferred with each other or with my technicians, and I went to my boss's office to complain, or to my office, or the ladies' room to cry.

Competence also became a tremendous issue for Ellen Howe, the warehouse manager: "It got so I could load the rail cars as fast as many of the men on my team. When I got new team members, I would load the car just to prove myself. But still, when I met someone new, I had to go through it all over again."

For black men, the problem of being seen as competent is equally acute. The issue for black managers as well as for women managers is that competence is not assumed, as it is with white males, but instead must be proved time and again. A senior black manager in a federal agency, Buford Macklin, said:

As a black manager it is much more difficult to be a logical thinker or a supportive manager because there's the feedback that you appear weak and indecisive. People expect black managers to come on strong and strident, and they don't seem to hear you unless you do. So if you expect to be heard at all, you almost have to be supermacho.

Price Cobbs, a psychiatrist and organization consultant, has seen more than 4,000 black managers participate in workshops offered by his organization, Pacific Management Systems, in San Francisco. He said of these issues in a recent conversation:

Contrary to contemporary mythology, or, more accurately, wishful thinking, many critical issues continue to confront black managers in the nonmulticultural environment of today's organizations. A process of corrections started after a generation of civil rights activities, the passage of laws, and good intentions. Today as yesterday, however, in most organizations, the causes of racial friction lie just beneath the surface seething and ever ready to explode.

Within organizations, a most difficult issue to confront and eradicate is that generated by institutional racism. It is abiding, manifestly unintended, and deeply imbedded in the structure of organizational life. It affects rewards and punishment, definitions of success, performance appraisal, and, in the value system, entitlements and natural selection of the "white male club."

Black managers continue to be the objects of racism. It is now perhaps more subtle than it was a generation ago, but for most Americans, there remains a core of individually held negative assumptions about Blacks. Within organizations this means that black managers all too often are viewed as filling jobs mandated by the government, as being less capable, and as occupying positions better filled by more worthwhile white males.

These twin strands of racism converge to present an unyielding front to black managers, relentlessly forcing them to adapt, adjust, and change while the organization and its people continue on with business as usual.

What is critical is change at both the organizational level and the individual level. Many white managers, as members of the majority group culture, are unaware of their one-up status. They do not understand to what extent Blacks are out of the information pipeline. What they take for granted in the way of access to information, resources, and power is actually available only to those in the mainstream of the organization.

The concept of androgyny, with its implications for interdependence and openness to feelings, holds out the possibility that white managers will begin to develop empathy for the black experience and come to understand the perks of their own majority status. Then, the door to change will really be opened.

Control: Who Drives the Car?

Women are not used to taking active control with men around. For example, women drive their own cars by day or night—unless they are with a man; then ritual takes over and many women relinquish control. In fact, many men report that they feel very uncomfortable having a woman drive the car. They even try to support this feeling with myths about women drivers. While such attitudes appear trivial, the implications must be faced if change is to occur.

Women have been valued as strong resources to be held in reserve, while men have taken direct charge. The image is so universal that if women take charge the perception is that they are uppity and aggressive. Research has demonstrated that there are rewards for different behavior on the part of women and men managers. For example, written case studies of management situations were given to managers and graduate students. They were asked to rank the effectiveness of the various managers in the studies. In one situation, Richard Jones, a new manager of a work team, entered an organization and spent three weeks interviewing employees and then developing a plan that spelled out how employees would operate. Jones was rated highly effective as a manager for initiating structure. When the name in the case was shifted to

Mary Jones but all the facts remained the same, the rating dropped to ineffective because Mary was too directive and pushy.

The prejudice of sex-role stereotypes works the other way too. A woman manager who spent time dealing with an employee with problems at home was rated effective for showing consideration for others. A male manager who exhibited the same behavior was rated wishy-washy for getting too involved in the needs of employees.[2]

Carol Gibson, the department head, began to be regarded as effective when she started adopting a masculine style:

> When I was promoted, there was a lot of concern from managers about whether it was right. I got superdefensive at the endless advice. Most of it was process advice. It was not until several months later that the mechanical manager, one of my peers, said, "You really pushed that issue and got it resolved. That was quite impressive." I beamed for an entire week. As I became secure in technical matters, I realized how I had stopped myself from sharing much of my personality with the men. I had focused almost exclusively on the task and had gone about my business without sharing my inner self at all.
>
> Five years later, I realized how boring and unapproachable I must have become. I decided to start letting them see more of me. Now, really for the first time, I feel more comfortable showing some of my feminine behaviors as well, instead of just focusing on the task. Just recently, after a meeting, I hung around to follow up with someone who did something in the meeting that was nonproductive. I really feel free enough to care about the person when I give my reaction. When I gave one colleague feedback, he got tears in his eyes. I feel so much less invisible now.

Dealing with Emotions

For women, expressing emotion is a particularly difficult issue in management circles. Men typically suppress emotion at work. If they allow themselves the luxury of expressing any feeling, it is likely to be anger. Indeed, in the experience of some women, men use anger as a weapon. Perhaps women sometimes use softer emotions in the same way.

In any case, emotional expression is important if men and women are to work effectively together. In this regard, men and women differ sharply. Women tend to see issues in the context of a total relationship, consisting of transactions between two people. The organizational style men have learned is a task-oriented one that responds more to the message than to the messenger. As a result, men are likely to feel isolated at work and to withdraw from expressions of feeling.

When asked how they feel about a woman's expression of dependency or tears, for example, men often describe it as "her problem." One said, "I usually try to help her be an adult and excuse her until she has finished crying." Another said, "I accept it as part of the situation and the other person's style of communication, which is different from mine." A few men said that they try to distinguish what they view as "manipulative" tears from "sincere" tears, and "tears of pain" from "tears of rage."

For women, dealing with emotions is a practical and poignant problem. Gibson, the department head, said:

> I would get so intense. I know it intimidated people, particu-
> larly some white males, who don't show their feelings a lot. I
> felt, with the maintenance organizations, that I was always
> trying to prove myself. As it happened, the technicians' respect
> came first, then the managers'. For the first four years, I felt I
> was paranoid about giving up my identity and generated a
> whole lot of anger toward the company. My anger seemed to be
> all I had to remind me I was me. I still worry that maybe I'm
> just buying into "their way" only because it is a lot easier to do.

Eventually Gibson could let herself become more androgynous, having proved herself first in the male arena. As she felt more secure, she became more effective by reintegrating her feminine behavior:

One of the reasons I've finally been accepted so well is because
I'm high on collaboration. There used to be a lot of staff and
line power squabbles. I was instrumental in introducing joint
accountability. People are working together much more in
harmony. I haven't done much hard charging. Mostly, I try to
get the guys to look at a variety of options, which is easier for
them. They really haven't had to deal with a strong woman who
controls them directly.

Ellen Howe, too, had to struggle with maintaining control over her
anger. At first she became unglued by the intensity of her feelings
and came across as quite aggressive:

There was a big battle over staffing. I thought I needed more
people on my team to get the job done. The other team leader
kept saying he could get the rail cars loaded with a reduction in
staff. I was pegged as the softie, but I believed what I said. I
can look back now and see myself ranting and raving and
making statements based more on feelings than on facts. It's
embarrassing to recall. I know how anxious I was that they
were going to say, "You're out to lunch," and that's just what
they did say. I was struggling so hard to share my feelings and
those of my team, but I didn't know how to do it their way.

I've changed my tone and approach a lot in dealing with
problems now and confronting situations. I'm much more diplo-
matic, and I can argue both sides. I used to say things like
"everybody," "always," and "never." Now I try to state the
arguments fairly so my message doesn't get discounted from the
start. It's such an uphill battle, but I feel like I'm making it.

Generally, the men I surveyed seemed uniformly wary of such
emotional displays as tears, rage, and fear. They often said that they
would like to be more supportive and adept in dealing with such
behavior, but that they generally responded with a variety of old
behaviors, ranging from withdrawal to lashing out. One man's
stance was typical: "I am usually very quiet and don't respond unless

her mouth keeps going. Then I become angry very fast." Women's verbal aggression frequently reminds men of childhood putdowns from mothers, teachers, or sisters.

As Richard Byrd, an organization consultant in St. Paul, said:

> One of the most difficult situations I have been in was with a woman client having a feminist crisis and hence projecting all her strong feelings on me. Under such circumstances, I usually either freeze and become highly rational or try to let the other person see the impact he or she is having on me. Neither approach worked with this client. Whatever I said was bad news. It was a Catch-22 situation.

Yet what emotions can men legitimately express in the marketplace? Frustration and mild anger seem acceptable in a number of organizations. Tenderness is another matter. Several male survey respondents spoke about how much they would like to reach out to friends going through the midlife crisis but were unsure of themselves and their emotions. "I wouldn't want to take it all on," said one. "I couldn't do justice to it, so I won't even start."

Dependency

If handling emotions at work is an important issue for women, learning to express feelings and dependency is a key issue for men. Dependency does not fit in with the stereotype of the supermasculine, supertough, super-self-sufficient American executive.

To study this stereotype, Fernando Bartolome, a professor at the Harvard Business School, interviewed 40 young executives and their wives.[3] The executives' average age was 37, and they had been married an average of 13 years. Nineteen were employed by large or medium-size companies, five by small companies. Seven were entrepreneurs, and nine were managers in organizations other than business. Nearly all the men (36) described themselves as seldom experiencing feelings of dependence. Also, the majority (32) ad-

mitted great reluctance to reveal feelings of dependence to their
wives when they experienced them. "Feelings of dependence are
identified as weakness or 'untoughness' and our culture doesn't
accept these things in men," said one executive.

Most of the men acknowledged that their expressions of tenderness were usually limited to members of their families, especially to
young children. And even displays of tenderness to children,
particularly boys, were inhibited by fear of "smothering" them or
making them too dependent on their parents. "Doing things is more
important than people," said one executive. "In skiing one only
needs man and hill; nobody else is necessary."

The men interviewed considered such character traits as
strength, self-reliance, and keeping a stiff upper lip as both masculine and conducive to success. One man commented:

> At work one gets accustomed not to express dependence and
> one does the same at home. As a matter of fact, at work I never
> think in terms of making good use of the available human
> resources. When I get home, I don't want to talk about any big
> problem: I just want to rest.

> I group my friends in two ways—those who have made it and
> don't complain, and those who haven't made it. And only the
> latter spend time talking to their wives about their problems.

Most of the men seemed to have abandoned any romantic views
they once had of their marriages. They had seen their marital
relationships turn from loving each other to partnerships in living.
They had seen their marriages lose their original charm and
intensity. In their jobs, these men sought and often found their
creativity, and sometimes a way of spending their lives without
being aware of too much pain.

Bartolome's study concludes that among men the values of
strength and self-reliance remain unquestioned, while the values of
toughness and controlled expressiveness are starting to be reconsid-
ered. This holds out hope for groundbreaking in the area of

emotional expressiveness for men, but it will probably be a long time before we see significant behavior change.

It has always been much more acceptable for women to express dependency than men. In fact, dependency has been so closely aligned with femininity that now women must work to get in touch with their beliefs and ideas rather than being so deferential and reactive. The Peabody Power Game, developed by George Peabody, is used as a simulation exercise in management development programs. Each participant receives four pages of instructions at the beginning. Sometimes a woman will frequently glance at the directions, put them down, turn to the person next to her, and ask, "What did they say?" Such a woman is undervaluing her own analytical capacity and instead is relying on someone else whom she assumes to have better skills.

Men sometimes unconsciously foster this feeling in women: One woman I spoke to found that her boss, who adopted her as a surrogate daughter, had difficulty with her as an employee when she tried to become more independent:

> I was hired for a very good job by a man who said, "I hired you because you are bright and because you have less experience than anyone else I interviewed. I can train you right." I was the only woman in the office and the only one to call my boss "mister." He approved my apartment before I signed the lease and warned me about dating various people. Then I got married, and our relationship seemed to fall apart. He started finding fault. Now I can see it was jealousy, but at the time I was confused and finally left the job.

In the organizational world it has frequently seemed safer for men and women to slip into parent-child (father-girl) relationships and for women and women to do much the same (mother-girl) rather than to meet each other as equals. Where men and women work together, all permutations of the model illustrated in Figure 2-1 could operate. But more often than not, the parental pattern seems to dominate. Male managers, for example, may call upon a woman

Figure 2-1. Preferred versus typical adult-adult
relationships in organizations.

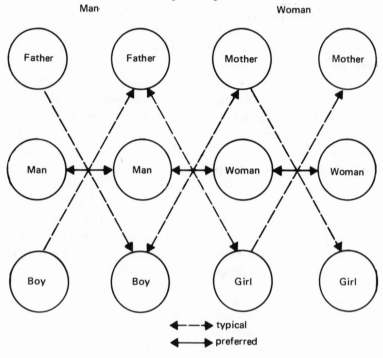

manager to "mother" a female employee who is crying. A woman
manager may ask a male manager for advice in areas where she is
fully competent. It seems the most difficult relationship to come by
in organizations is the adult-adult model. That opens the door to
issues to be discussed further in Chapters 12 and 13.

The antecedents of parent-child relationships run deep. Men
have been socialized to protect and provide to the point where, in the
words of one male consultant, "I found it difficult to just go with my
colleague's momentary feelings of inadequacy without striving to
find a solution for her." Women have been socialized to nurture and
climate-set. Much has been written about the treatment of profes-

sional women as mothers, office wives, hostesses, and mistresses. My survey indicated that women are most concerned with being treated as little girls by dominant, either paternalistic or emotion-depriving men. Several said expressions of cool withdrawal or dispassionate, logical thinking are particularly upsetting and remind them of their relationships with their fathers. They thought their job status most precarious when they were discounted as children in a "big people's" atmosphere.

Intimidation and humiliation, actual and anticipated, were often mentioned as women's worst interactions with men and the most threatening to their fragile sense of themselves as serious, adult professionals. Typical responses when asked to fantasize about such toxic interactions included:

"Having my ideas, suggestions, and opinions ignored."

"A lot of putdowns."

"An argument with another manager that I thought would come to blows in front of other people."

"A man could undermine my position by treating me as a child, calling me 'girl' despite my protestations."

"I could be hit, as I almost was once."

Women generally found that when they were treated like children, it was all too easy for them to respond as children. Those who successfully dismantled the parent-child syndrome have learned responses different from those they used at home.

One woman, the only female professional in a small organization where feelings were openly expressed, told me:

The staff meetings were often full of raised voices and vigorous attacks on one another's ideas and actions. We aired a lot of feelings but also expressed a lot of mutual caring. So it wasn't unusual for the president of the firm, who had a hot temper, to raise his voice to any of us. However, little by little I realized I was becoming the recipient more often than the men and usually not even regarding my actual work—just heated statements like, "Shut up a minute and let me finish."

For a long time I virtually pulled my tail under, said nothing, and felt guilty and embarrassed, as I would have had this been my father. Finally, I noticed that the men were more confronting, coming back at the president in a firm voice, and combatting his behavior. At one staff meeting, I tried the same tactic, raising my voice to counterattack, "Don't you talk to me that way!" He was so stunned that he later offered me a warm apology and never again vented his anger at me. Much to my surprise, we established an effective, professional, rewarding relationship.

The experience of jointly working out the emergence from dependency can be important for both men and women as well as for the organization. Howe described the process as follows:

When I started working in manufacturing five years ago, my boss saw me as his daughter. He changed a great deal in our time together. He started answering my questions in an adult way. He used to scold me while I was in training. Those three months of training were so painful. He would grill me each week about what I had learned. He would ask me what we should change each week. I didn't know. It was such a new world that I just had to concentrate on learning the process. I was so afraid of telling him what I didn't know. For my part, I learned a lot about putting my feelings into words so they wouldn't overwhelm me or him. I used to just cry or get angry or walk out of the room like I couldn't control myself—like a little girl. Then I began to force myself to stand there and say what I was feeling. It got less scary. I could cry and talk at the same time. I stopped seeing him like an overpowering father. I started taking more responsibility for myself. I put my head and my heart together more. I guess I was trying to be androgynous.

Later, he acknowledged he really didn't know how to deal with me. In 25 years, he had never had to deal with a woman manager. When I cried, it was too unfamiliar to him. We worked so hard on our relationship. He cared a whole lot and learned so much. Eventually the company asked us to meet with the new boss–woman manager duos and talk with them about our evolution. We were amazed at how helpful we were to them. My boss died last year of a heart attack at the age of 55. I miss him a lot.

NOTES

1. Eileen Morley, "Women's Thinking and Talking," Harvard Business School Case No. 9-477-055, Harvard Case Clearing House, Boston, Mass. 02163.
2. Kathryn M. Bartol and D. Anthony Butterfield, "Sex Effects in Evaluating Leaders," *Journal of Applied Psychology*, Vol. 61, No. 4 (1976).
3. Fernando Bartolome, "Executives as Human Beings," *Harvard Business Review*, Vol. 50 (November–December 1972).

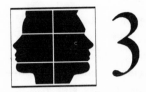

3

Management
and the
Concept of Androgyny

For the past 50 years, the functions of management and the roles of managers have been the subject of a great deal of literature and debate. The classical school of management, prevalent from the turn of the century until World War II, set out clear principles of scientific management, work scheduling, and work simplification in order to increase efficiency and output. Accepted management principles included division of work, unity of direction, unity of command, subordination of individual interest to general interest, centralization, a clear chain of command, and orderly arrangement of personnel and material.

The human relations school, which began in the 1920s, recognized the existence of an informal organization that supports personal needs and motivation and interpersonal work group relations. They added the notion that management's function is to get work done through others in a complex social environment that contains many variables, including peer relations, working conditions, and boss-worker relations. In the process, they focused almost too heavily on the psychology of individual workers and not enough on the interaction among group members.

In 1960, Douglas McGregor, a management theorist, urged managers to abandon assumptions that employees work only for economic reasons, want little responsibility, and require close supervision. Greater dedication and effectiveness would come from the assumption that workers desire meaningful work and greater autonomy, McGregor argued.[1]

The management science school, developed in the 1960s, stressed the use of technical resources and skills. It relied on such tools as quantitative methods and computer analysis to solve problems and plan for the future. Decision making was aided by mathematical models and theoretical constructs, such as linear programming and Program Evaluation and Review Technique (PERT).

Recently, the field has shifted away from an exclusive focus on managing work. Instead, it is generally agreed that the two most important managerial functions are concern for task (initiating structure, or a production orientation) and concern for people (showing consideration for others, or an employee orientation). The shift in thinking has come about because of the realization that there is a strong interaction between managing work and managing people—that human factors have a major impact on organizational effectiveness. Paul Hersey and Kenneth Blanchard, professors and consultants in the field of organizational behavior, have defined management as "working with and through individuals and groups to accomplish organizational goals."[2] That is quite a human definition for the technocracy in which we now work.

If, indeed, the management of people is as important as the management of task, then effective managers need to acquire and value both instrumental ("masculine") and expressive ("feminine") behaviors. Broadly speaking, these might be characterized as rational problem-solving and analytical skills, and as nurturing, helping, and interpersonal skills. Managers who develop a combination of masculine and feminine behaviors will be able to employ a full range of management styles as they work to develop and empower, as well as to lead and evaluate, employees.

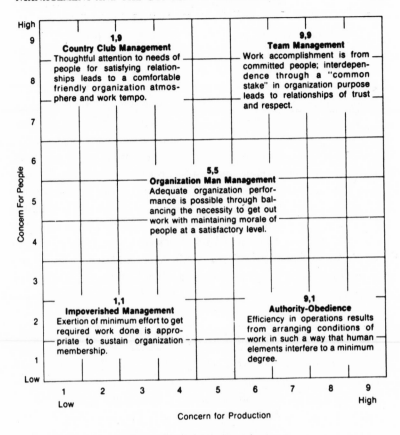

Figure 3-1. The Managerial Grid.*

The Blake-Mouton Managerial Grid (shown in Figure 3-1) maps managers' styles into five categories on the basis of their degree of concern for people and production.[3] The 9,9 "team builder," with high concern for both people and production, is the preferred style. It emphasizes the development of interdependent, trusting work groups that are committed to achieving organizational goals. The 1,1

*From *The New Managerial Grid*, by Robert R. Blake and Jane Srygley Mouton. Houston: Gulf Publishing Company, copyright © 1978, p. 11. Reproduced by permission.

"do nothing" manager shows low concern for both people and task. The 1,9 "country club" manager cares strongly for people but much less for task. The 9,1 "production pusher" has high concern for task but not for people. A 5,5 rating indicates a middle-of-the-road manager—"the organization man." Once again, the importance of people skills as well as production skills is emphasized by this model.

Today's managers are being tossed about by conflicting demands and needs. Human resources management promotes collaboration and democratic leadership, open communication, personal trust, and participation. Yet in many organizations a manager is more highly valued for independent thought, self-reliance, a competitive spirit, and aggressive leadership. Since these traits derive mostly from male socialization, female managers are caught in a double bind. If their managerial behavior reflects organizational values, they may be regarded as "not feminine enough." If they follow the "feminine" model, they may function far below their managerial capacity.

Traditional Management Functions

As the models described above suggest, traditional functions associated with masculine behavior work best when they are carried out with a blend of feminine skills in handling the interpersonal dimensions of work. The interrelationships between masculine and feminine behavior can be shown by examining the long-accepted functions of management: planning, organizing and coordinating, staffing and motivating, and directing or controlling. These operations reflect classical management theory and its guiding principles of scientific management. They deal explicitly with the arrangement of work and supervision, but only implicitly with concern for employees.

Planning, for example, deals with defining and obtaining goals. Planning activities include forecasting, establishing objectives, programming, scheduling, budgeting, and developing policies and procedures. Managers need analytical and intellectual skills to break projects into component parts, determine resource allocations, and schedule complex activities. However, to get the data necessary to develop goals and criteria for judging if the goals are attained, managers need to consult their subordinates. Ideas and suggestions from those closest to the work can test whether the plan is realistic. Employees who feel free to be creative about objectives are most likely to offer assistance. Planning requires a shift, then, from independent analysis by managers to collaboration with employees. Here is where feminine alliance-building skills come into play: effective managers need to open communication, explore alternatives, negotiate differences, and build consensus with subordinates. Many management-by-objectives systems have suffered, not from lack of clarity about the objectives but from lack of ownership of the objectives. If communication is not open in the course of developing objectives, the results will be rigid, uncreative, unilateral goals. Management cannot be effective in the long run if those who know the work and the problems are not involved in the planning process.

Organizing brings together financial, human, and capital resources to meet management goals in the most effective and efficient way. Increasing emphasis is being placed on coordination, as managers enter the greatest era of interdependence in the workplace in history. Entirely new functions have been created in coordination. For instance, the U.S. Department of Housing and Urban Development has an assistant secretary for management coordination. A shipbuilding firm has a top position of manager of ship coordination. Aerospace corporations play coordinating roles between government agencies and private industry. Coordination requires both alliance-producing (feminine) and compliance-producing (masculine) skills. It calls for both collaborative and directive behavior. (See Figure 3-2.)

The staffing and motivating function determines the level of performance. This function deals with how well individual and organizational goals will be met. Staffing extends beyond hiring and work assignment to the responsibility for developing employees on the job and evaluating their performance. It covers recruiting,

Figure 3-2. Management competencies.

Masculine	Neutral	Feminine
Instrumental behavior	Command of basic facts	Expressive behavior
Direct achievement style	Balanced learning habits	Vicarious achievement style
Analytical problem-solving, decision-making, and judgment-making skills	Continuing sensitivity to political events	Accommodating skills
	Quick thinking	Self-knowledge
		Creativity
Proactivity—inclination to respond purposefully to events		Social skills
		Nonverbal sensitivity
		Alliance-producing skills
Visible impact on others		Mediating skills
Negotiating skills		
Compliance-producing skills		

hiring, coaching, developing and training, and creating incentives for motivating employees. Maintaining staff requires candid feedback about employees' strengths and weaknesses, the establishment of trust to promote open discussion of professional and personal goals, the development of networks, and the ability to give advice and support for employees' developmental needs.

Too often the approach to staffing is almost random. One male founder-president of a California electronics firm told me:

> Hiring people is the toughest thing I do. I'm operating strictly on gut feelings when it comes right down to it. I only wish I had more intuitive ability. There have been tremendous disasters, all hinging on my intuition. Now everybody hired is on a three-month probation at first. This gives me a little more latitude in finding out if my intuition is on target.

Controlling requires that managers compare goals and objectives and match up resources with the desired results. It calls for analytical skills, clear judgment, and the ability to gather accurate data. Top managers in one large government agency were asked to list their areas of responsibility. Many enumerated 40 different functions. Then they learned that they would be evaluated on performance in each area. As they took a closer look under the threat of accountability, they were able to shorten their lists. Some managers could find only two areas that they controlled directly. Interdependence was so tight that most managers were exclusively responsible for only a few functions.

Traditional Motivational Roles of Managers

Managing both program and human resources needs is the complex job of every manager. It creates a tension that the manager can never fully dismiss. The manager's goal is to have employees maximize their personal contribution to the organization and, simultaneously, to have the organization improve individual satisfaction from work.

What personal needs must the organization respond to if it wants to increase productivity, develop people, and retain employees? One model has been suggested by Michael Maccoby, a psychoanalyst involved in social psychiatry. Maccoby set forth four principles for increasing employee effectiveness in organizations: (1) security (worker freedom from fear and anxiety over the necessities of life); (2) equity (compensation commensurate with contribution to the value of service performed or product produced); (3) individuation (stimulation of craftsmanship, autonomy, and learning); and (4) democracy (participation by workers, as opposed to authoritarian control).[4] In his consulting work with senior managers at the Department of Commerce, Maccoby has encouraged the development of boss-subordinate human effectiveness/organization effectiveness contracts.

David McClelland, a psychologist at Harvard, specifies three major interpersonal motives: the need for achievement, the need for affiliation, and the need for power.[5] The achievement need is related to personal standards for success and is met best in organizations where leadership is based on expertise rather than on position. The need for affiliation speaks to the need for comfortable, rewarding relationships with others and is met best in organizations that encourage expressions of warmth and support and joint problem solving rather than criticism and blaming. The need for power is based on the desire to influence or control others and is facilitated in organizations that share leadership rather than allowing a few to dominate. People have different degrees of need in these areas and can be trained to increase one motive (such as achievement) over another. In addition, people are motivated to fulfill their needs in different ways. Those with high achievement needs may seek out greater challenges and work of greater social significance, but may not change their behavior to establish closer social relationships with co-workers. Others may work hard when they are enjoying affiliation with peers but may be reluctant to strive for impact or control.

What is important to remember is that motivation shifts as the environment changes. The 1960s were characterized by achievement motivation. This fact is difficult to recall, since we have moved into an era where power dominates. We have yet to see a time when affiliation permeates the national scene, although flower children offered us a naive glimpse for a while. Furthermore, there are sex-role bases for the expression of these needs. For example, it has been more or less acceptable for women to appear to be motivated more by affiliation than by power; and the reverse has been true for men.

Power, according to McClelland, is the desire to have an impact through taking strong action, producing emotions in others, or acquiring a reputation.[6] McClelland describes several ways of gaining a feeling of power:

1. A person may feel strengthened by an outside source of power, such as working for a powerful person or, for some, taking drugs or alcohol.

2. A person may become more powerful by accumulating possessions, such as cars, jewelry, and credit cards—all of which may be considered extensions of the self. Or a person may engage in body-building exercises or a strict diet to feel more self-control.

3. A person may compete through persuading, bargaining, manipulating, or helping others. Helping is power-oriented because the receiver often feels that he or she is weaker than the giver. Helping, in this case, is difficult to distinguish from alliance-producing behavior. In their research on families, Joe Veroff and Sheila Feld at the University of Michigan found that in the middle and upper classes fulfilling power needs is a strong motive in childrearing and spouse relationships.[7] Academicians have a strong power motive to the extent that they are gratified by developing the critical thinking capacities of their students, who come as suppliants to the fount of knowledge.

4. A person may see himself or herself as an instrument of a higher authority. Religious leaders and politicians fit this category; so do scientists, for whom the higher authority may be the laws of science.

Richard Boyatzis, president of McBer & Co. in Boston, developed a two-factor theory for affiliation.[8] Those managers with high "affiliative assurance" needs tend to be less successful because they are concerned with the security of their close relationships. Anxious about recognition, they are often jealous and possessive about relationships with subordinates and bosses. They frequently have difficulty placing goals in perspective when interpersonal issues are at stake.

In contrast, managers with high "affiliative interest" needs tend to enjoy close relationships and gain energy from other people. They thrive on the camaraderie of a community at work or at home and are quite effective in motivating those around them because of the high respect they communicate to others.

Jean Lipman-Blumen, a sociologist, and Harold J. Leavitt, a professor of organizational behavior at the Stanford Business School, have done research on achievement styles.[9] One style, which they call a vicarious achievement ethic, describes people who define their identities through their relationships with others. These people "feel they have won or succeeded when someone they are close to has succeeded." Such people feel a sense of accomplishment when they contribute to the success of a spouse or child at home or when they provide support to co-workers at work.

The other style, a direct achievement ethic, describes people who "select, initiate, and seek out activities that permit a direct confrontation with the environment." They are attracted to winning, gaining power, and solving problems as means to ends—which may include building relationships and getting others to love them. Both styles are necessary in the workplace—to get work done and to develop people. A direct achievement style may be quite effective when change is needed. But during a period of consolidation, a vicarious achievement style may be more effective.

Concern for Interaction of Task and People

The dual concern for task and people has a strong foundation in contingency theory, as stated by Fred Fiedler, a psychology professor at the University of Washington. Fiedler holds that there are three aspects to management: (1) manager-subordinate relations; (2) the degree of structure in the task; and (3) the position and power of the manager.[10] Managers juggle their concern with task and people on the basis of (1) their own interpersonal skills; (2) the needs of their subordinates; (3) the maturity of the work team; (4) the clarity or ambiguity of the task; (5) the degree of interdependence required to do the work; and (6) their position and degree of personal power in the organization.

Managers can respond to changing expectations by varying their leadership style to meet employee needs, organizational needs, and the nature of the work to be done. This means that organizations must adopt structures that blend technical and personal segments of the system. In any given situation, managers need to adopt the style that best achieves the organization's goals though its employees. This type of "contingency management" requires an androgynous blend of directive, collaborative, and participative skills.

For example, the manager faced with a pressing deadline or unanticipated crisis may need to exercise independent decision making, impose structure, and exert authority. If this firefighting mode becomes habitual, however, it would seem that something is wrong with the system. In contrast, planning for a merger or developing a long-range goal requires a more participatory approach in which people feel free to share their ideas, to take risks, and to collaborate by building on each other's visions.

Effective contingency management calls for the development of both masculine and feminine characteristics. Men may need to trade competition and authority for collaboration and compassion when faced with workers who can best be motivated by teamwork and personal development. Women may need to assume more assertive, autonomous postures· when work requires quick decisions and structured leadership. In short, both men and women need to avoid rigid adherence to any one style and should watch for changes that call for different patterns of management behavior.

New Views of Management Functions

"The consequences for society of the imbalance between the development of technical and social skills has been disastrous," wrote Elton Mayo, a founder of the behavioral school of management.[11] Mayo understood that book learning would not develop effective managers, and his critique still has currency. Studies by the American Assembly of Collegiate Schools of Business show that MBA programs develop managers who possess concepts but not skills. To date, a practitioner-oriented, competency-based MBA program does not exist. However, the seeds of a definition of management competencies are developing in areas. For example, managers are being trained in interpersonal concepts at seminars and conferences, such as the Menninger Foundation Executive Seminar, the American Management Associations management seminars, and the National Training Laboratories Institute Management Work Conference. This is an important trend, encouraging managers to look inward and to attend to their personal needs. Formats range from dissemination of literature on stress to workshops in life planning. There are also courses in acquiring assertiveness skills and in applying scientific work standards and measurements.

Today's managers need to adopt a broad approach, focusing on:

- Scientific and technical competencies (the ability to use the information, techniques, and material needed to perform the tasks).
- Interpersonal and social competencies (the ability to work with and through people).
- Environmental competencies (the ability to relate to the outside world, establish policies, and develop relationships with constituencies).

Managers also need to assess their own attitudes and behavior, evaluate group or organizational performance, and, finally, interact with constituencies, government representatives, and the public to solicit their ideas.

Management Dimensions in the 1980s

People are at least as important in management as programs and products. Henry Mintzberg, management professor at McGill University, substantiates this point through his observations on how managers do their work. He describes three major sets of roles that are the building blocks of managerial functions: the informational roles, the interpersonal roles, and the decisional roles—all of which have a strong interactional component.[12]

The *informational roles* call for the manager to act as monitor, spokesperson, and disseminator. The manager receives, translates, and transmits a vast array of information from inside and outside the organization. The motivational function of this role is crucial to good management. Since communication is central to management, the manager must be able to communicate so that people are motivated and the work gets done. More is required than just logic or the ability to persuade.

The *interpersonal roles* include a variety of functions. Here the manager acts as:

- A figurehead who represents the organization externally by performing symbolic duties and routine responsibilities that must come from the top.
- A liaison who maintains a network of useful outside contacts and information sources.
- A leader who hires and motivates employees and oversees their training and development.

Therefore, the manager must be skilled not only in the technology of programs and services and the conceptual realm of planning and organizing, but also in the subtleties of personal interaction and human behavior.

The *decisional roles* include the functions of the entrepreneur, the conflict manager, the resource allocator, and the negotiator. The manager must initiate and design projects and project improvements, commit financial and human resources (negotiate budgets and determine salaries), devise strategies for handling unexpected problems, and negotiate for the organization. In short, the manager sets objectives, gathers information, evaluates alternatives, and takes action.

A new dimension of management is emotional competence, described by Edgar Schein, professor of management at the Massachusetts Institute of Technology. Combined with analytical and interpersonal competence, it is essential to effective management. Schein defines these three competencies as follows:

Analytical competence: the ability to identify, analyze, and solve problems even without complete information.

Interpersonal competence: the ability to influence, supervise, lead, manipulate, and control people at all levels of the organization to achieve organizational goals more effectively.

Emotional competence: the capacity to be stimulated, rather than exhausted, by emotional and interpersonal crises, to bear high levels of responsibility without becoming paralyzed, and to exercise power without guilt or shame.[13]

Today's managers need to strike a balance between personal attitudes, emotions, and expressions and those qualities that promote more effective work relationships. They need to be well schooled in the masculine dimensions of self-reliance and independent decision making as well as in the feminine interpersonal skills of being trustful and open and possessing self-awareness. Human needs cannot be understood nor human resources developed unless the organizational climate is one that allows vulnerability and dependency to be freely expressed. Such a climate can lead to the discovery of strategies that motivate employees and foster their career growth.

NOTES

1. Douglas M. McGregor, *The Human Side of Enterprise* (New York: McGraw-Hill, 1960).
2. Paul Hersey and Kenneth H. Blanchard, *Management and Organizational Behavior: Utilizing Human Resources* (Englewood Cliffs, N.J.: Prentice-Hall, 1969).
3. Robert R. Blake and Jane Srygley Mouton, *The New Managerial Grid* (Houston: Gulf Publishing Co., 1978), p. 11.
4. Michael Maccoby, *The Gamesmen: The New Corporate Leaders* (New York: Simon & Schuster, 1976).
5. David C. McClelland, *The Achieving Society* (New York: D. Van Nostrand, 1961).
6. David C. McClelland, *Power: The Inner Experience* (New York: Irvington Publishers, 1975).
7. Joseph Veroff and Sheila Feld, *Marriage and Work in America* (New York: D. Van Nostrand, 1970).

8. Richard E. Boyatzis, "The Need for Close Relationships and the Manager's Job," in David Kolb, Irwin Rubin, and I. McIntyre, eds., *Organizational Psychology: A Book of Readings*, 2nd ed. (Englewood Cliffs, N.J.: Prentice-Hall, 1974).
9. Harold J. Leavitt and Jean Lipman-Blumen, "A Case for the Relational Manager," in *Organizational Dynamics* (Summer 1980), pp. 27–41.
10. Fred E. Fiedler, Martin M. Chemers, and Linda Mahar, *Improving Leadership Effectiveness: The Leader Match* (New York: John Wiley & Sons, 1976).
11. Elton Mayo, *The Social Problems of an Industrial Civilization* (New York: Arno Press, 1977).
12. Henry Mintzberg, *The Nature of Managerial Work* (New York: Harper & Row, 1973).
13. Edgar Schein, *Career Dynamics: Matching Individual and Organizational Needs* (Reading, Mass.: Addison-Wesley, 1978), pp. 135–136.

 *4*

What Androgyny Means to Men and Women

The case for the androgynous manager thus far largely rests with an appeal for increasing the behavioral options of managers in order to help them manage people more effectively, reduce stress, increase motivation, and respond to differences among individual workers. However, this does not explain how androgyny might affect the men and women who embrace it as a personal vision and try to encourage it throughout their organizations.

People have an enormous personal stake in making these professional changes, since they have implications both at home and at work. Their impact is bound to increase as more and more men and women look beyond stereotypical sex roles to define their own behavior and interpret that of others. The result may be a great deal of initial discomfort, as with any social change. People will be practicing behaviors foreign to their early teaching and ongoing socialization, and they will have problems readily accepting unaccustomed behavior in others. Androgynous behavior is not yet the predominant mode taught by parents, teachers, or the media.

In 1979 Louis Harris and Associates surveyed the values, attitudes, and goals of American males 18 to 49 years old for a *Playboy* magazine report. The survey analyzed male attitudes regarding "family life, love and sex, marriage and children, the 'outer man' and 'inner man,' drug use, money, work, politics, and leisure."

Personal interviews were conducted with 1,990 men, from a cross-section of economic levels. The men were shown a list of 11 basic values and asked to rank the importance of each to them personally. The results in order of importance were as follows: health, family life, love, friends, sex, respect for others, religion, peace of mind, work, education, and money.

Yet if one were to ask for a behavioral index of how these men actually spend their time, the focus would undoubtedly be on work, television, sports, and perhaps education. The men's belief in the importance of family life is not supported by their time commitments or their ways of sharing themselves. Slightly less than half the men surveyed (49 percent) described sex as being "very important" for their personal happiness. Only about half the men said they were "very satisfied" with their sex lives. Again, many men are not spending their time developing their intimate relationships.

Nevertheless, there is a great potential payoff, both in and out of the workplace, for men and women to expand the roles they now assume. In reality, the comfort of playing out established roles is at best questionable. Do men really feel alive in the traditional male role, when they rarely let down their guard as aggressive competitors? Are women comfortable when the deferential qualities they practice so well become barriers to their advancement in the workplace? The promise of androgyny is that both men and women will be able to behave as whole, integrated people at work and at home; that they will no longer have to compartmentalize their needs and behavior; and that they will enjoy satisfying relationships with members of their own sex as well as with each other.

Women as Androgynous Managers

Perhaps the greatest significance of androgyny to women in management is that it can help them resolve the discrepancy between their feminine socialization and the perceived masculine characteristics required of managers. Currently, female managers face a variety of barriers, stemming both from within themselves and from others. Not the least of these is that they are seen by others as bringing "female" qualities to the office when "male" qualities are felt to be the characteristics of good management. Androgyny, if adopted by men and women as the most effective management strategy, may help resolve the dilemma by redefining characteristics of management to include a great many that have heretofore been prescribed as "feminine."

Research supports the notion that women are perceived to have far fewer managerial characteristics than do men. Virginia Schein, a consultant on organizational behavior, used samples of male and female managers to show that managers of both sexes believe successful managers in general to possess characteristics, attitudes, and temperaments ascribed more commonly to men than to women.[1]

Masculine characteristics associated with managers in Schein's studies include leadership ability, competition, self-confidence, objectivity, aggressiveness, forcefulness, ambitiousness, and desire for responsibility. Feminine attributes associated with managers were intuition and such employee-centered behaviors as understanding, helpfulness, humanitarian values, and awareness of others' feelings. Perceptions of competence, intelligence, persistence, tact, and creativity were not related to sex. Summarizing her findings, Schein noted:

> All else being equal, the perceived similarity between the characteristics of successful middle managers and men in general increases the likelihood of a male rather than a female being selected for or promoted to a managerial position. To the

extent that a woman's self-image incorporates the female sex-role stereotypes, this relationship would also seem to influence a woman's job behavior. Given the high degree of resemblance between the perceived requisite management characteristics and characteristics of men, women may suppress the exhibition of many managerial job attributes in order to maintain their feminine self-image. However, for certain managerial characteristics not synonymous with the masculine sex-role stereotype, women presently may be more readily acceptable. In certain situations, exhibition of these stereotypical feminine behaviors may be advantageous.

Not only are some men and women reluctant to have a woman boss but, more seriously, they prefer to work with a man. In a Department of the Navy study on preferred co-workers, the characteristics of an androgynous co-worker were chosen as the most desirable, "masculine" characteristics were second, and "feminine" characteristics were the least desirable.[2] Nonetheless, when asked directly, both men and women indicated they preferred male co-workers. The perception frequently seems to be, and rightfully so, that a man has access to more information and will be more in touch with power people, listened to more by others, and in a position to make better decisions. Such expectations demonstrate the long road ahead in altering stereotypes and including women as full citizens in the workplace.

It is unlikely that our perceptions of management characteristics will change quickly. However, it is essential that women striving for management success develop those so-called masculine traits that are perceived as making successful managers in general. Only in this way will others believe in their potential and grant them the confidence and resources necessary to achieve success. If women are perceived as possessing only feminine managerial abilities and lacking the masculine qualities considered synonymous with successful management, they are unlikely to be taken seriously or to be given the tasks and support necessary to become first-rate managers.

As women take it upon themselves to demonstrate androgyny, it is likely that they will make others aware of the value of feminine as well as masculine management traits. To date, regrettably, women have more readily acquired the masculine style of competition and forcefulness and limited their expression of intuition, interpersonal understanding, and sensitivity.

In fact, one of the greatest quandaries that managerial women will face in the coming years is how much they must give up in order to gain professional success. It is extremely difficult for women to retain feminine characteristics when they are advancing in organizations as a result of their ability to demonstrate masculine traits. As an assistant personnel director in a large city government agency said of his female boss: "She knows how to get ahead. She's ambitious and does all the right things politically in the organization to get herself lots of visibility, even though her technical knowledge isn't really exceptional. I don't find it difficult to work for a woman, but then I never think of her as a woman."

Androgyny provides an answer demonstrating the value of masculine *and* feminine traits working in tandem. As more and more people embrace the concept of androgyny, characteristics from both ends of the sex-role spectrum will become respected management capacities, and women will no longer find it necessary to give up their "feminine" behaviors as they acquire characteristics more typical of men.

Men as Androgynous Managers

We begin with the basic assumption that the biological sex differences, such as the tendency toward more rough-and-tumble play and higher activity level in boys,[3] will not inhibit either sex from increasing its androgynous behavior. Psychologists and biologists give great weight to both nature and nurture in the development of sex typing. But as Norma McCoy, a psychologist, says: "The clear message is that even if biologically based sex differences in behavioral predispositions exist, social factors such as the sex which the child is assigned and in which the child is reared can substantially override and obscure them."[4] While this is a complex issue, it is clear that, whatever the effect of biological differences, our behavioral options are seriously limited by the socialization process. Being born male or female has an enormous impact on our self-concept and on what other people expect of us and how they react to us. In the same way, being born white or black or brown is one of the primary determinants of our life experiences and of how others react to us.

From birth on, boys are allowed more independence than girls. In early childhood, they are encouraged to express more aggression than girls. As they enter college and career, success does not conflict with their sex-role expectations. Boys are taught competition and problem-solving skills in concert with organizational demands. They learn camaraderie among those teammates who can help them win the game. They practice a tough style; the predominant emotion allowed to them is anger. Fear and pain are practically denied expression.

Men have not been as aware as women have of the implications of sex-role stereotypes, since they are so in the middle of the problem that they usually can't see it. Charles Ferguson, in *The Male Attitude*, notes, "I could not find where men watched themselves even out of the corner of their eyes behave as males. It was always that men seemed wholly unaware of the sex origins of their ideas."[5]

According to Robert Townsend, professor of English at Amherst College, it is extremely difficult for men to give evidence of how and why their lives are *men's* lives, what values inform them, what they are thinking and feeling because they are men, or what in the void makes them behave as they do. It is difficult for men to recognize the limitations and privileges conferred on them because they are male. Men have yet to attempt a definition of "we"—of what "our" imagination is; what "our own" literature is like; how "our" physical and political power have determined what we write about; just how "we" have imagined, catered to, patronized, adored, and oppressed women; just what fears and loathing have motivated "us"; what "we" may be or have been when we had the confidence to take ourselves for granted.[6]

Joseph Pleck, one of the major forces in the men's field and currently at the Wellesley College Center for Research on Women, says relationships between men need to be reexamined with similar acuity to what the women's movement is doing for women. According to Pleck, men often perceive no emotional alternatives to the relationships they feel themselves losing with women, and this may contribute to the panic the current women's movement has aroused in many men.[7] But the other side is scary too. As one man said, "I have a pretty good idea what I can get in a relationship with a woman, but I just don't know with a man. I guess I have to try to find out."

One more example: D. H. Lawrence's admonition to men was "Nothing matters. Everything happens. One wants to keep oneself loose. If you get held by anything, break it. Don't be held. Break it, and get away. Don't get away with the idea of getting something else—just get away for the sake of getting away. Beat it!"[8]

Many men, however, are becoming aware of the effects of sex-role stereotyping and are starting to reassess their relationships. Now, with the increasing emphasis on the management of people and on the concerns of the new workforce for personal satisfaction on the job as well as outside work, men are questioning whether adherence to all things masculine is worth the pressure and the harm to their health—and whether "masculinity" itself is even effective behavior. In increasing numbers, men appear willing to risk some standard symbols of professional success in order to achieve a lifestyle that better reflects their personal desires and needs.

There is substantial evidence that men are finding traditional male managerial qualities confining and limited, even though these qualities are equated with success and men have been accustomed to developing them from an early age. Men are also dissatisfied with their competitive job climate. When pressed, they express discontent with the grinding competition that cannot give way to more comfortable forms of collaboration. Many feel trapped by their traditional behavior patterns and dissatisfied with the relationships these patterns produce.[9]

In this case, androgyny provides an important answer for men by increasing their options for behavior. As men become more intuitive, sensitive, and collaborative, they will be able to enhance their managerial skills as well as to achieve more comfort in all aspects of their lives. And as organizations come to value androgyny, men may be relieved of some of the pressures of unflagging competition and tough-mindedness.

How long it will take for men to broaden the range of their behavior remains an important question. Part of the problem is that men frequently see androgyny as a form of diminished identity rather than as a way of expanding their personalities. They feel that it means they must give up part of themselves, part of their "masculinity." In certain professions, however, men have achieved an understanding of the value of an androgynous style. Lewis Young, editor-in-chief of *Business Week*, recently said in *The Washington Post* (November 4, 1980): "In the communications business you've got to have that stimulative, emotive kind of leadership. You can't order someone to write a good story." Zubin Mehta, head of the Israeli Philharmonic and the New York Philharmonic, described his role of conductor as part godfather, counselor, father confessor, and coach.

Adopting the concept of androgyny does not mean that men and women (or male and female managers) will come to behave exactly alike. When the door is opened and we are all free to select beyond sex-role stereotypes, a whole new range of behaviors will be possible—and each of us will be free to choose our own blend.

Sex Roles in Groups

There are significant differences in how men and women behave when working with the other sex or the same sex in a group situation. This diversity of behavior can only mean that at certain times people's behavior changes according to circumstances rather than according to individual characteristics.

An early study of sex-role differentiation in groups shows that in mixed groups men are more active in taking the initiative and getting on with the task.[10] In addition, men's contributions in groups are more highly valued by others—even above the contributions of those women who do assume active, initiating roles.

Both men and women tend to ascribe lower status—and thus lower potential for contributions—to women. Women typically defer to men in group decision making, following men's lead and agreeing to their suggestions. Highly dominant men and women tend to become leaders in groups of their own sex, but in mixed groups dominant women will usually defer leadership to men (whether these men are high- or low-dominant types). One body of research showed that in mixed groups highly dominant women were willing to make the decision about who should be group leader, but the decision they usually made was that the leader should be a man.[11] The conclusion is that the same old behavior predominates: women tend not to assume leadership when men are present.

In an interesting study of this phenomenon, Marlaine E. Lockheed, researcher at the Educational Testing Service, demonstrated that the average man initiates many more acts in mixed groups than in all-male groups.[12] This is why mixed groups in general tend to be more active than same-sex groups. It was also found that when a woman feels she is competent at a task and has had an opportunity to test this in an all-female group, she will have the confidence to be more active in mixed settings.

Studies of work accomplished in mixed groups generally indicate that such groups are preferable to all-male or all-female groups. It was also found that problem solving in mixed groups is superior to that in single-sex groups.[13] The conclusion was that women in all-female groups do not seem to have the high motivation for problem solving shared by all-male groups and that all-male groups are more likely to let competition interfere with problem solving.

Mixed groups, on the other hand, seem to achieve a level of motivation and coordination that facilitates problem solving.

Elizabeth Aries, professor of social psychology, has shown that in male-female groups men talk twice as much as women do.[14] The content of all-male groups differs from that of all-female or male-female groups. All-male groups tend to be competitive and impersonal; all-female groups tend to deny power issues and to focus on personal themes. Mixed-sex groups are likely to be a combination of both.

That women can have an ameliorating influence on the competitiveness and hostility that often arise in groups has been demonstrated in many instances. College administrators found that coed dorms were damaged less than all-male dorms and that the presence of women in the dorm tended to cut down on the rowdiness of men. Women and men both reported more natural relationships as a result of the coed experience. In the same vein, in the workplace managers have reported a decrease in problems of rowdiness and arguing when women have been added to an all-male team, such as a motor pool in a federal agency.

The challenge of androgyny in group settings is for both men and women to recognize the value of bringing masculine and feminine qualities to a group. In this way, the group can draw upon a rich mix of skills to accomplish tasks and undertake group processes. To achieve such a goal, women need to believe in their own abilities to contribute, and men need to strive for collaboration and process.

Because men now predominate in the marketplace, it appears that their ratification of androgynous behavior is more significant than women's. But it is critical—and not an easy next step—that women be on board to support the change in men.

NOTES

1. Virginia Ellen Schein, "The Relationship Between Sex-Role Stereotypes and Requisite Management Characteristics," *Journal of Applied Psychology*, Vol. 57, No. 2 (April 1973).
2. Kirsten Hinsdale and J. David Johnson, "Masculinity, Femininity, and

Androgyny: What Really Works at Work?" ONR Technical Report No. 2, Contract No. N00014-77-C-0625. U.S. Office of Naval Research, Washington, D.C., September 1978.

3. See John Money and Anke A. Ehrhardt, *Man and Woman, Boy and Girl: The Differentiation and Dimorphism of Gender Identity from Conception to Maturity* (Baltimore: Johns Hopkins University Press, 1972).

4. Norma L. McCoy, "Innate Factors in Sex Differences," in Alice G. Sargent, ed., *Beyond Sex Roles* (St. Paul: West Publishing Co., 1977), p. 166.

5. Charles W. Ferguson, *The Male Attitude* (Boston: Little, Brown, 1966).

6. Robert Townsend, "The American Male: His Values and His Voids." Unpublished manuscript, 1977.

7. Joseph Pleck, "Is Brotherhood Possible?" in Nora Glazer-Malbin, ed., *Old Family/New Family: Interpersonal Relationships* (New York: Van Nostrand Reinhold, 1974).

8. D. H. Lawrence, *Phoenix II: Uncollected, Unpublished, and Other Prose Works*, collected and edited by Warren Roberts and Harry T. Moore (New York: Viking Press, 1968), p. 366.

9. Barbara Bunker and Edith Seashore, "Power, Collusion, Intimacy-Sexuality, Support: Breaking the Sex-Role Stereotypes in Social and Organizational Settings," in Alice G. Sargent, ed., *Beyond Sex Roles* (St. Paul: West Publishing Co., 1977).

10. F. L. Strodtbeck and R. D. Mann, "Sex-Role Differentiation in Jury Deliberation," *Sociometry*, Vol. 19 (1956).

11. E. I. Megaree, "Influence of Sex Roles on the Manifestation of Leadership," *Journal of Applied Psychology*, Vol. 52 (1969).

12. Marlaine E. Lockheed, "The Modification of Female Leadership Behavior in the Presence of Males." Paper presented at the American Educational Research Association meetings, Washington, D.C., March 1975.

13. L. R. Hoffman, "Group Problem Solving," in L. Berkowitz, ed., *Advances in Experimental Social Psychology*, Vol. 2 (New York: Academic Press, 1966).

14. Elizabeth Aries, "Male-Female Interpersonal Styles in All-Male, All-Female, and Mixed Groups," in Alice G. Sargent, ed., *Beyond Sex Roles* (St. Paul: West Publishing Co., 1977).

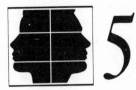5

Increasing Androgynous Behaviors

There are already signs that men and women want to expand beyond their sex roles. In the process they describe a sense of awkwardness about trying out nontraditional, nonstereotypical behaviors. Some women are concerned about being "too masculine," and some men are afraid of appearing indecisive. Women in assertiveness training sessions claim, "I'd like to be more forceful, but I'm afraid people will say I'm pushy." Men in interpersonal awareness courses say, "My wife has suggested I be more tender and expressive, but when I try it just seems awkward." Recently, I was approached by some women leaders in a federal agency who wanted "aggressiveness training"!

Many successful managers would agree with a male executive in a large public interest organization in Washington, D.C.:

> I can see that my style creates some barriers to a close team
> feeling on my staff. I'd like to get closer to people myself, but I
> never have been able to. I guess I don't have the courage to take
> that on. If I tried getting closer and it didn't work, we might
> actually end up with less communication than we had before,

65

and attempts to get closer to people could take a lot of time away from regular work.

Any change, even that which we impose upon ourselves, brings with it large doses of self-doubt, questioning, and disorientation. Maybe everything we do is not perfect, but at least the imperfections are comfortably predictable. Ellen Goodman, columnist and author, has studied how the changing sex roles in America have affected people's lives. She presents the quandary this way:

> What fear of loss makes one person hesitate at a turning point? What conflicting values are inherent in the choices another finds too difficult? What hopes for the future prompt someone else to embark on a risky course? What meaning is invested in the status quo, what meaning is invested in change? There is a part of us that finds change exhilarating and full of hope and a part that fears the disruption and loss it brings. [1]

Increasing Behavioral Options

The change to an androgynous management style requires the development of a new range of skills, not necessarily the elimination of existing skills. Certain skills, however, such as competitiveness for men and deferential behavior for women, may have been overlearned and need to be practiced less. Thus there is time for a phasing-in period—experimenting with "masculine" and "feminine" interpersonal competencies while becoming comfortable with them. The androgynous manager is still engaged in planning, organizing, directing, controlling, and all the other functions related to organizational life, but is free to draw upon a greater range of skills to accomplish these.

Instrumental and Expressive Behavior

There are two broad categories of behavior: instrumental (problem-solving, or objective) and expressive (interpersonal, or subjec-

Figure 5-1. A comparison of instrumental and expressive behavior.

Description	Instrumental Behavior	Expressive Behavior
Purpose	Problem solving: to avoid failure, to achieve success	Self-expression: to get acknowledged, to get connected
Exchange	Services; information	Empathy
Basis	Data	Feelings
Needs served	Control; power	Spontaneity
Time orientation	Future-oriented; planned	Spontaneous
Structure	Predictable, certain, clear, agreed-upon, negotiated, con-tracted	Flexible, ambiguous
Avoid at all costs	Surprise	Boredom

tive). These have been described by Peter Block and Neale Clapp, consultants at Block-Petrella Associates (see Figure 5-1). Most organizations value instrumental behavior almost to the exclusion of expressive behavior. Yet it seems impossible to hold developmental sessions with employees; have planning meetings where participation and creativity are valued; deal with employees going through major transitions in their lives; reduce stress in the workplace; have effective boss-subordinate relationships; and solve the issues surrounding declining productivity, without utilizing both instrumental and expressive behavior.

In order to begin increasing their options, managers need to assess their current personal style. The assessment scale on the following page, developed by Charles Seashore, a consultant in Washington, D.C., lists key dimensions of personal style and demonstrates the range of possible behaviors for each. The absence of certain skills means less freedom to use the most appropriate style to get one's needs met in a particular situation.

Some Dimensions of Interpersonal Competence

The points on each of the scales below represent skills which may range from very well developed on the one hand to never practiced on the other hand. There are no values attached to the different points, as the skills at each point may be appropriate in certain situations. The power of the individual increases to the degree that he or she can freely select from a number of possible different points on each scale in any situation. These scales may be used to identify strengths or underdeveloped skills, to give feedback to another person, or to clarify expectations.

1. Leadership

Take command	Help others take command	Compromise	Follow command	Rebel against taking commands

2. Visibility

Center stage	On stage	Backstage	Observe at a distance	Be absent

3. Conflict and Confrontation

Generate	React to	Mediate	Ignore	Avoid

4. Connectedness

United	Intimate	Teammate	Distant	Isolated

5. Helper/Helpee

Express vulnerability	Take suggestions; get feedback	Share support	Give help	Rescue others

6. Self-Disclosure

Disclose self	Hint at Openness	Present façade	Hide	Disappear

7. Limits and Controls

Set and keep strong limits	Suggest limits	Develop limits	Test limits	Break limits

8. Group Size and Ease of Participation

Large groups	Small groups	Pairs and couples	Individuals	Alone

Use the scoring system below to identify the range of situations in which you feel comfortable and then to identify the particular situations in which you would like to develop a given skill:

0 — if you don't have this skill
+ — if you have this skill
X — if you could improve

Behaviors Specific to Sex Roles

Certain behaviors reflect sex-role stereotypes and therefore limit the development of effective management styles in particular situations. Many experts agree that there are different patterns of behavior characteristic of men and women. For example, Allen Ivey, developer of the business and counseling microskills training programs in Amherst, Massachusetts, notes:

> Informal analysis of thousands of interviewing sessions suggests that indeed men and women do differ in their typical patterns of communicating. Men tend to be more intrusive; they ask more questions and give more advice and direction. Women, on the other hand, tend to use more passive communication skills, such as reflective listening. Further, men tend to use more active language (e.g., "I did that to him"), whereas women will regularly use more passive language (e.g., "He did that to me"). Recent research has substantiated these informal observations and validated our early impressions.

It is difficult to distinguish those behaviors that represent you and your desire to manage competently from those that reflect a pattern of sex-role socialization. The following questions can help you make this distinction.

Primarily for Women

○ Do I rely on suggestions by others at the expense of my own ideas?
○ Do I take personal credit for my successes or consider them just lucky?

- Am I willing to take on a tough assignment with no help from others?
- Am I willing to risk failure by working in areas where I am uncertain of my abilities?
- Am I reluctant to be forceful about accomplishing tasks because people might not be happy with this approach?
- Do I have compliance-producing skills as well as alliance-producing skills with employees?
- Do I assert the authority of my position to get things done as much as I think I should?
- Do I spend too much time counseling and sympathizing with employees about their personal needs, and do they come to me too often with their needs?
- Do I appear to be so vulnerable that others are reluctant to be candid with me?
- Do I express my feelings so openly that others sometimes feel uncomfortable around me?
- Do I freely share ideas and suggestions, even when I suspect they may meet with disagreement?
- Do I have both men and women in my support system?
- Do I quickly back down on arguments when others don't seem to agree with me?

Primarily for Men

- Do I insist on an independent, can-do-it-alone approach to complex problems that may benefit from others' input?
- Am I competing when collaboration is more appropriate?
- Am I sensitive and empathic in my discussions with employees about their needs?
- Do I have a good support system of peers who give me accurate feedback about my behavior?
- Am I able to demonstrate dependence and vulnerability when that is how I feel?
- In meetings and planning sessions, do I push for task accomplishment at the expense of group cohesiveness and sharing?

- Does my desire for career achievement sometimes get in the way of other goals and needs in my life?
- Do I tend to dominate and control in most group situations?
- Do I feel I have lost if I don't win others over to my point of view?

Pointers for Men

To develop an androgynous style, most men need to concentrate on the following areas: developing the ability to express personal feelings even when they may expose vulnerability or dependency; promoting close interpersonal relations through open and honest communications, including listening and feedback; valuing work for its ability to provide self-fulfillment and affiliation with others as well as career achievement; and accepting emotion and spontaneity as healthy personal qualities to be explored and expressed. Some specific pointers for development in these areas include:

1. *Communicate*
   - Listen empathically and actively but without feeling responsible for solving others' problems.
   - Learn to use nonverbal communication more—use physical contact; give warmth and approval through touching. The sexual implications of such behavior call for caution and negotiation. But at home children and spouses may be wishing for more pats and hugs as signs of caring.

2. *Express feelings*
   - Become aware of, accept, and express tender as well as tough feelings.
   - Regard feelings as an essential part of life and as guides to becoming a fully functioning person, rather than as impediments to achievement.
   - Accept and express the need to be nurtured when feeling hurt, afraid, vulnerable, or helpless, rather than hiding these feelings behind a mask of strength, rationality, and invulnerability.
   - Share feelings as a meaningful part of your contact with others, accepting the risk and vulnerability that sharing implies.

3. *Examine attitudes*
    o Accept the vulnerability and imperfections that are part of all people.
    o Assert the right to work for self-fulfillment as well as to be the provider.
    o Value an identity that is not defined totally by work.
    o Learn how to fail at a task without feeling you have failed as a man.
    o Personalize experience, rather than assuming that the most valid approach to life and interpersonal contact is objectivity.

4. *Deal differently with men*
    o Build support systems with other men, sharing competencies without competition and sharing feelings and needs.
    o Allow close friendships to develop with men.
    o Confront homosexual fears so they do not inhibit closeness with men.

5. *Exhibit expressive behaviors*
    o Nurture and actively support other men and women in their efforts to change.
    o Give up performance-oriented sexuality for a more sensual, less goal-oriented sexuality.

Pointers for Women

Women typically need to work on directing the accomplishment of tasks more forcefully; tempering their expression of feelings with appropriate use of logic and analysis; promoting themselves within an organization by becoming more visible and entrepreneurial; and making their opinions known clearly without backing down in the face of possible disagreement.

1. *Communicate*
    o Develop skills in self-expression, using body posture, vocal tone, speech rate, and eye contact to communicate not only a desire to be helpful but also clarity about your boundaries and your willingness to say no.

- Learn to state exactly what you want and face the risk of being cut down or wrong, especially at meetings. This is not a "safe" position, but it is an honest one. Be concerned more about stating your own position than about how the other person is reacting to you.
- State your own needs and do not back down, even if the immediate response is not acceptance.
- Learn effective feedback. Indicate to others that you heard accurately what they said; disclose your own thoughts and feelings directly; leave an opening for negotiation between the two positions—but then question feedback, do not just swallow it.
- Stop self-limiting behaviors, such as allowing interruptions or laughing after making a serious statement.
- Make "I" statements. Make many more statements with you as the subject rather than the object of the sentence. The present tense and active voice are more risky, but they have more impact than the passive voice.

2. *Take action*
   - Practice taking risks and overcoming fear. Men typically subordinate feelings and fears to action. Women in a problem situation may cry before they take action and lose considerable time in the process. It is difficult to learn to cry and talk at the same time, but it is certainly preferable to crying and being unable to talk, or crying out of anger and not recognizing it.
   - Learn to focus on a task and regard it as at least as important as the relationships among the people doing the task.
   - Be entrepreneurial.

3. *Examine activities*
   - Stop turning anger and blame inward. Stop making negative statements about yourself. Make positive statements about yourself and adopt a highly competitive, masculine power style in the process.
   - Stop feeling comfortable with being a victim and suffering.

4. *Deal differently with women*
   - Develop an "old girl" network, working more closely with other women. Such a network opens up contacts for women and offers them an opportunity to share information about what jobs are available, what's going on in the organization and around town, and how to get their needs met.
   - Build a sense of community among women instead of saying, "I pulled myself up by my bootstraps, so why can't she?"
   - Support other women to the same degree or more than women support men.

5. *Increase problem-solving and analytical skills*
   - Get appropriate training in decision making, analytical skills, and assertiveness.
   - Learn to formulate models and to generalize from a number of experiences. Sometimes women are reluctant to discuss the big picture because it makes them more visible and vulnerable. It seems necessary to risk being wrong, at least with people who know you well.
   - Get into management development programs or support systems with men to test out abstract models and share your diagnostic thinking.

The current assignment of sex-role expectations underutilizes skills in both men and women. The division of labor as it stands now requires that men and women pay a high price in order to hold on to their sex-role designations. Acquiring a broader range of behaviors helps managers of both sexes work more effectively, particularly in utilizing the management style most appropriate to a given situation.

NOTE

1. Ellen Goodman, *Turning Points* (Garden City, N.Y.: Doubleday, 1979).

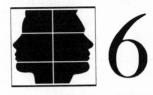

New Models of
Effective Managers
in the 1980s

The time for moving toward more androgynous modes of managerial behavior seems particularly ripe. Forces within the workplace are making the old, predominantly masculine style of management counterproductive. Human resources management is emerging as a major field. Policymakers see their capital resources shrinking in a tight economy; they realize they must attend to the human contribution to organizational goals if they are to improve efficiency and work output. Workers themselves no longer join organizations just for a paycheck, but increasingly seek self-fulfillment and a sense of personal contribution through their work. The intense focus on technology in the 1980s requires a catch-up in the human arena; some industries are experiencing a lag between their employees' capacities and motivation and the level of sophistication of their equipment.

We are looking today at a complex reality in management: (1) declining resources; (2) a new set of worker values; (3) a new workforce comprised more than ever before of women and minorities, whose needs require different management skills; (4) individual and organizational desires to reduce work-related stress; and (5) a recognition that the old-style management by experience is naive for today's world and must be replaced with effective managerial coaching and well-designed management development programs. This chapter will examine some of these trends and their implications for the 1980s.

New Worker Values

Daniel Yankelovich, professor of psychology at New York University and head of the attitude research firm bearing his name, writes at length on the changing values among workers. In exchange for loyalty and hard work, employees want more than just a job, more than just money, more than just security. They want work that provides them with an opportunity for self-expression, a sense of challenge, a chance to give service, the right to do a whole job and not just part, real involvement in the decision-making process, true identification with their employers and co-workers, and a chance to contribute to society. According to Yankelovich, we see these new attitudes arising

> . . . in many negative forms within the present work population: in the angry, sometimes unreasonable demands of union workers; in widespread withdrawal of interest in work, as evidenced in higher turnover and absenteeism rates, cheating, shrinkage and the like; and in a kind of managerial obsolescence whose primary cause is a sense of being excluded, a feeling of meaninglessness, and a disaffection with work and career, and whose primary symptom is lack of motivation. What is probably meant by "lack of motivation" is a lack of organizationally acceptable motivation. Nowhere is this disaffection more pronounced than on production lines, where workers often do only one simple operation.[1]

Yankelovich concludes that the values of the new breed of workers indicate a growing focus on psychological well-being as well as on economic security. When work fails to provide such psychological benefits, people dedicate themselves more to personal satisfaction outside the workplace and less to a commitment to organizational goals.

Yankelovich explains the importance of the refusal to subordinate personality to work role:

> People will often start a job willing to work hard and be productive. But if the job fails to meet their expectations, if it doesn't give them the incentives they are looking for, then they lose interest. They may use the job to satisfy their own needs but give little in return. The preoccupation with self that is the hallmark of new breed values places the burden of providing incentives for hard work more squarely on the employer than under the old value system. . . . Perhaps the chief lesson we should draw from the changes shaped by the new values is that concern with the human side of enterprise can no longer be relegated to low-level personnel departments. In the 1980s, knowledge of how the changed American value system affects incentives and motivations to work hard may well become a key requirement for entering the ranks of top management in both the private and public sectors.[2]

Responses to these needs are slowly beginning to emerge in those organizations that have established quality circles or worker rap groups in order to increase employee involvement in product quality, build workers' sense of ownership in the enterprise, and foster greater commitment to productivity.

New Management Skills

The changes in worker values described by Yankelovich suggest that the competent manager of the future will need a new set of skills and that the nature of management itself will change significantly. Likely changes in management in the future, as described by John McHale and Magda Cordell McHale, include:

○ A shift from hierarchical, authority-oriented managerial forms to more participative structures.
○ A shift from tactical or short-range to strategic or long-range management.
○ An increase in the participatory role of community and consumer groups.
○ A shift in the basis of authority from economic coercion to consent of the managed.
○ A rejection of management by experience and a higher regard for the field of management.
○ A shift of attention from management by others to self-management.[3]

The change in management style is particularly evident in the personnel function. Personnel departments are working on building partnerships with line managers to increase their effectiveness in their dual responsibility as developers of human resources. "The most difficult function of the personnel department is to develop new approaches to matching personal and organizational goals. There must also be general conviction for a tough-minded as well as warm-hearted approach—and [a conviction] that from the satisfactions of people with their jobs flow improved morale, greater productivity, improved competitive position, and larger profits," Yankelovich writes.[4]

Donald N. Michael, professor at the University of Michigan, provides the following guidelines for future management skills— what he describes as the "new competence":

○ The ability to live with and acknowledge high uncertainty and change. We will no longer be able to control because the variables are so many and often unknown. There are no longer simply technological solutions to many of our problems.

- The ability to continue to learn. If we claim to know everything, people will not believe us.
- The capacity to embrace errors, expecting them and treating them as learning experiences rather than as failures, and thereby engendering trust and openness.
- The need for future-oriented responses. We need to have goals and visions.
- The interpersonal skill to respond to diversity and to nurture differences, made more urgent by the presence of a changing workforce.
- The capacity to know ourselves. We need to know our contradictions, our vulnerabilities, and our strengths, and how and why we will take risks.
- The cultivation of personal and organizational support systems.[5]

If the issues of management in the future portrayed by McHale and Michael are to be dealt with, management values and practices must change. The traditional organizational style will have to yield and soften. Crispness, aggressiveness, and sharpness are too narrow a range of skills and must be blended with receptiveness to others' needs and values if managers are to be responsive to the complex tasks they face today.

Managers need the traditional skills of planning, organizing, and directing as well as the new interpersonal competencies. Open communication is essential for feedback, cooperation, and participation, and is critical for planning and strategic management. Continued give-and-take gives workers a sense of shared responsibility and ownership in the enterprise. This will be crucial in the turbulent times ahead, with scarce resources available to solve complex problems. Only through a blend of masculine and feminine behaviors can managers effect the fit between individual needs for autonomy and interdependence and organizational goals.

Finally, a manager needs to be a participant-observer—that is, to become involved and to observe that involvement in order to reflect on others' choices for behavior. The manager must know how to diagnose a problem and determine the best approach to it—whether that involves clarifying roles, defining goals, or refereeing a turf battle. Management development helps a manager understand that problems do not always have easy solutions. One such problem is that of integrating the individual and the organization. There is not an easy one-to-one fit. Rather, it is a dilemma to be reckoned with, and the dynamic tensions between personal and organizational objectives need to be juggled.

Management Development and Education

Surprisingly few organizations have comprehensive management development programs that are focused on different levels of management: new managers, middle-level managers, and executives. The exemplary programs are at the Federal Executive Institute in Charlottesville, Virginia; General Electric in New York; IBM in Armonk, New York; and Xerox Corporation in Lessburg, Virginia. David Lasey at the Insurance Company of North America in Philadelphia has developed a program for several levels. Disney University in Anaheim and McDonald's University in Chicago serve primarily to orient employees to the business rather than to develop management skills.

Lou Willet Stanek at Philip Morris developed "influence managing" to teach upper middle managers how to influence employees whom they don't hire, fire, or control in order to gain their cooperation. Philip Morris has a career development program that focuses on values clarification and skills identification. Employees attend these sessions before they enter any other training program.

One of the most well-developed training programs is the Managing People Program at Citibank. Thirty-nine "managing people principles" were developed at Citibank through interviews with employees about the critical competencies for human resources management. These principles are used in training programs for middle managers and executives. A few examples are listed below.

Getting commitment to goals and standards: you communicate high personal standards informally (in conversation, personal appearance, and so on).

Coaching: you build warm, friendly relationships with the people in your work group, rather than remaining cool and impersonal.

Appraising performance: you communicate your views honestly and directly during discussions of staff members' performance.

Compensating and rewarding: you use recognition and praise (aside from pay) to reward excellent performance.

Managing staff for continuity of performance: you conduct work group meetings that increase trust and respect among staff members.

Even though the needs of managers are recognized by many corporations, they are generally not clearly enumerated. It is a critical task today for organizations to assess the needs of managers by (1) describing expectations for each level of management, from new manager to middle manager to executive; and (2) getting managers to assess their own learning objectives and developmental goals.

Many organizations have contracted the assessment function to outside firms. These assessment centers attempt to identify managerial potential, using a series of exercises that simulate actual managerial problems. The centers evaluate the candidate's performance on such criteria as setting priorities, delegating, and making decisions. In the last ten years, the list of companies using the assessment method has grown from a few hundred to nearly 2,000. Yet according to ArDee Ames, director of the Special Programs Consulting Division at the federal government's Office of Workforce Effectiveness and Development, "To spot effective managers, assessment centers need some criteria about what makes an organization effective, and these criteria are largely lacking at the present time."

Even management schools do not have a clear set of management competencies for different levels of management. Warren Neel, dean of the College of Business Administration at the University of Tennessee, fears that the professional schools may be producing a "cadre of technocrats" who lack the ability to communicate and to deal with interdisciplinary problems.

Most MBA programs teach theory and analytical skills through the case method but are not concerned with producing graduates who have the attitudes, values, knowledge, skills, and competencies necessary to be practitioner-managers. The American Assembly of Collegiate Schools of Business, which accredits 204 business schools in the United States and Canada, set up a task force to review the situation. The group is to report on whether criteria for accreditation should include the ability of a business school to turn out graduates who can handle stressful situations as well as master accounting principles.

Development of Managerial Competencies

The development of managerial competencies is a long and complex process. Among the best sources of data are skilled managers who view their work as a craft. Unfortunately, many managers cannot clearly describe what their role is and what they do. It is important to get these managers to explain how they manage, how they step back and gain a perspective on their organization, and how they maintain a participant-observer posture and keep track of long-term goals.

The balance of skills needed at different levels of management has been categorized by Robert Katz, of the University of Michigan Survey Research Center,[6] as follows:

Level of manager	Conceptual skills	Human skills	Technical skills
Top	47%	35%	18%
Middle	31%	42%	27%
First-line supervisor	18%	35%	47%

An elaboration of the skills required for the executive level has been developed by McBer & Co. in Boston. The company explored characteristics of many corporations and public sector agencies that led to effective performance and identified various sets of managerial competencies. However, as Richard Boyatzis, president of the firm, points out, the competencies must be framed in the language of the particular organizational culture. The definition of a given competency (such as team building) varies greatly with the organizational style.

A sample competency list from McBer is described below. It appears with a complete set of characteristics in Richard Boyatzis' forthcoming book, *The Competent Manager*.[7] The competencies break down into five categories: knowledge, entrepreneurial skills, intellectual abilities, emotional maturity, and interpersonal abilities. The total blend includes areas that have been stereotyped as either masculine or feminine. Acquisition of these competencies makes a manager more human as well as more effective.

Knowledge Competencies

Managers need a command of basic facts and the relevant professional knowledge, such as engineering, personnel, budgeting and procurement. Knowledge competency is not sex-role related, although the manner in which the knowledge is used may be.

Entrepreneurial Skills

Entrepreneurial drive indicates a concern for unique achievement and the improvement of a process. The entrepreneurial manager is continuously interested in cutting down time and expense. This often is associated with productivity and includes goal-setting and planning skills.

Entrepreneurial managers are proactive. They use their problem-solving and information-getting skills to keep on top of the situation rather than reacting to events. In order to look ahead, managers must believe that situations can change. Those who are not proactive tend to see situations as insuperable and are not successful in coping with difficulties. Proactive managers take the initiative when something goes wrong and try to anticipate problems that may arise. Proactivity is primarily masculine (instrumental) behavior, part of a direct achievement style.

Intellectual Abilities

The successful manager uses his or her mind as a tool to get things done. Conceptual ability is needed to see thematic consistencies in diverse information. This inductive process includes the capacity to organize diverse information and to communicate insights. Logical thinking is required to develop the major policy themes the manager has identified. A manager must be able to assess the importance of the themes and the arguments that support each one. Logical thinking includes the ability to understand cause and effect: if a particular theme is pursued in a specific manner, certain consequences can be expected. The manager also needs a good memory and an ability to think deductively. Because women managers may be reluctant to put the models for their thinking out front, they may appear to behave in a highly reactive fashion and to be lacking in conceptual skills.

Emotional Maturity Competencies

Emotional maturity competencies include three that have stereotypically been considered masculine: self-control, perceptual objectivity, and stamina. Self-control is the ability to keep personal feelings or desires out of a reaction. Even under the domination of feelings or impulses, the person with self-control can differentiate between essential and nonessential battles. If completing the task is the goal, then managers must be able to sidestep a thorny interpersonal issue that is irrelevant at the time. However, managers also need to stay in touch with the feelings they are overriding. Without an awareness of spontaneous feelings, managers are likely to become rigid and to lack the responsiveness that is so critical to work relationships.

Perceptual objectivity is another important emotional competency. If the manager's viewpoint is contaminated by biases emanating from power or affiliation needs, he or she is not free to examine the merits of an issue. By the same token, if the manager's perception is distorted by reactions to the messenger, the response to the message cannot be made objectively.

For obvious reasons, a good manager also needs stamina and high energy.

Interpersonal Abilities

The "feminine" side of androgynous management emerges most strongly in interpersonal skills. The effective manager has presence —that impressive quality that makes people listen when he or she speaks. Presence is an amalgam of many qualities: self-confidence and self-knowledge, a desire to lead, an understanding of what is needed and wanted, and a desire to communicate. The manager with presence is highly focused in energy and has a commitment to the development of others. He or she is able to establish rapport with others and to make them feel valued. Counseling skills help the manager tune into the feelings of others and assist them in expressing those feelings.

The desire and ability to influence are important characteristics of effective managers. Managers want to have an impact on what happens, and they are not afraid to use their influence to make things happen. Good managers use their position power to produce compliance and their social power to build networks or alliances.

Effective managers also speak clearly and persuasively. They have a concern for relationships and value people. They are sensitive to the feelings and points of view of others and can respond appropriately. In the managerial world, social sensitivity stems more from a concern for being effective than from a concern for being empathic for its own sake. The employee who feels rejected, put upon, or put down will not be fully committed to helping the organization accomplish its goals.

Finally, managers need to be effective with groups, to be able to get people to collaborate and feel a sense of team spirit—a goal that requires primarily feminine (expressive) behaviors.

Other competency lists are given in Appendix B. A description of self-assessment instruments available for measuring androgynous behavior is presented in Appendix C. It must be reiterated that competencies are much more effective when they utilize the language of a particular organizational culture.

It is not difficult for an organization to develop its own competencies, utilizing some of the samples presented here and tailoring the language accordingly. What the model of androgyny offers is a screen to place over the competencies so that they are responsive to both the current and the future needs of managers.

NOTES

1. Daniel Yankelovich, "The Real Meaning of the Student Revolution," *Conference Board Record*, Vol. 9, No. 3 (March 1972).
2. Daniel Yankelovich, "The New Psychological Contracts at Work," *Psychology Today*, Vol. 11 (May 1978).
3. John McHale and Magda Cordell McHale, "Management: The Larger Perspective," in Edward B. Rusk, ed., *Challenge to Leadership: Managing in a Changing World* (New York: Free Press, 1973).
4. Yankelovich, "New Psychological Contracts," *op. cit.*
5. Donald N. Michael, *On Learning to Plan and Planning to Learn* (San Francisco: Jossey-Bass, 1973).
6. Robert Katz, "Skills of an Effective Administrator," *Harvard Business Review*, Vol. 52 (September 1974).
7. Richard E. Boyatzis, *The Competent Manager*. Manuscript in preparation, 1980.

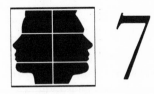

7

Androgyny and Management Systems

Numerous signs indicate that organizations throughout the country are shifting toward management systems that call for feminine as well as masculine behaviors. Industry and government are re-examining structures that reflect patterns of hierarchy and control. They are questioning the value of competition, autonomy, power, and tough-mindedness in light of the interdependence that work now requires. Workers' shifting attitudes toward their jobs are having an effect as well. Management research now offers a new set of practices aimed at increased productivity. These practices require more interpersonal ability, more collaboration, more interdependence, and more open communication—all of which point to an androgynous blend of skills.

Among the major objectives of modern managers are: (1) to raise the level of employee motivation and effectiveness in order to increase productivity; (2) to increase the readiness of peers and subordinates to accept change; (3) to improve the quality of all managerial decisions; (4) to develop teamwork and improve morale; and (5) to further employees' development so that managers succeed each other smoothly.

Matrix management, management by objectives (MBO), and other management systems are being utilized to meet these ends. Yet many of the managers responsible for implementing these systems come from highly technical disciplines and lack the skills to make the systems effective. All too frequently, managers brought up under a system that stresses the rational, exclusively task-oriented aspects of work are not well cast to play the complex human roles required by today's systems. These new approaches call for much more inter-dependence, negotiation, role clarification, and participation than directive, top-down methods do.

By the time a practice like management by objectives or job enrichment has gained popularity, a myriad of articles in business journals have appeared analyzing why the fad has failed. The new management approaches take much longer to implement than many systems designers realize. Systems planners, line managers, training directors, and others often do not have the opportunity to work as a team to diagnose needs, plan for change, and adopt the model to the needs of those most affected by the system. Before people are asked to change *what* they do, they must be taught *how* to do it differently.

This chapter examines three important approaches that have a bearing on the development of the new style of management: management by objectives, matrix management, and performance management. Other significant approaches, such as career planning and organization development, are covered in the following chapter. Research has demonstrated that managers who implement the new systems most effectively have a blend of masculine behaviors (setting high standards and expectations for themselves and others) and feminine behaviors (being receptive to and concerned about the people who assist them in accomplishing their goals).

Restructuring Organizational Processes and Functions

Managing Work—Management by Objectives

Ideally, in MBO, manager and employees jointly identify com-mon goals, define each person's major areas of responsibility in terms of the expected result, and use these as measures to guide the operations of the unit and to assess the contribution of each unit member. Before goals are defined, attention is paid to group makeup, group processes, and team building. MBO is a valuable strategy by which both managers and subordinates can control organizational missions and goals. Organizations have found MBO a powerful tool for building commitment toward shared goals, ranging from improved productivity to individual career development.

MBO's major thrust is to clarify the objectives of each person's job and of the work team so that progress can be monitored and evaluated. It also tests how these objectives fit into larger unit and overall organizational goals. The MBO cycle may include (1) team building; (2) defining organizational goals, objectives, and measures of performance; (3) negotiating an agreement between employer and employees about goals and measures; (4) checking interim results against milestones; and (5) revising original goals as necessary.

MBO focuses on program objectives as well as on objectives that relate to the needs of employees, such as finding dignity in meaningful work. As such, MBO calls for a range of managerial skills, from planning and evaluation to open communication and interpersonal effectiveness. Under MBO, the manager who once could drop paper appraisals in a subordinate's in-box must now meet that subordinate face to face to set objectives, assess progress, and evaluate results.

MBO can lead to greater openness between employer and employee and to increased teamwork through collaborative efforts to clarify the goals to which individual objectives contribute. Many organizations have taken steps to ensure meaningful participation for employees who are expected to achieve the objectives. For example, MBO may include training in group process and collaborative problem solving. Many employees lack adequate background in interpersonal skills and are not as comfortable, open, or effective in groups as they are working alone or in one-on-one relationships. The goals of training are to help all employees be more at ease working in groups and to encourage an androgynous mix of managerial skills, blending both analytical and interpersonal competencies.

Matrix Management

Matrix management superimposes the management of individual projects on the traditional functional system and thereby establishes a multiple command system, with employees working for at least two bosses. Under this system, specialists from relevant functional areas work together to tackle problems that cross functional lines. An example is the matrix organization developed at Harvard Business School, whereby faculty are members of both academic departments and program areas (master's program, executive program, and so on).

The space program had a great impact on organizational design and helped to spawn matrix organizations. Project management developed primarily because many organizations found it necessary to establish temporary intact systems. Thus, at the National Aeronautics and ·Space Administration, employees report to both a project (or program) manager and a functional manager (such as administrative services).

Project teams address distinct problems: researching a special project, developing a new product, installing a new plant, or initiating a new system. Numerous projects, under different project managers, may exist in varying stages of completion at any given time. Managers in the various functional areas supervise the "talent bank" for project teams and determine the availability of skills for various projects. Team members may return to their functional specialties or transfer to new project teams when a project is completed.

Obviously, competitive win-lose or solo-contributor behaviors are in opposition to the teamwork required in a matrix organization. Team members need to share responsibility at daily meetings and work cohesively with other units in the organization. To be effective, the matrix system requires collaboration, openness, and a problem-solving rather than a blaming approach.

A top-level executive with 33 years experience in a *Fortune* 500 chemicals company that recently shifted to a matrix system described the change in words quite supportive of androgynous behavior:

> The entire company has, in the past two years, changed radically in order to go to a matrix management system. This definitely is requiring more of what has been termed an "androgynous" style. Managers are finding that they need to work more closely with people and to be more reflective. The people doing well under our matrix system are those who are able to bring more sensitivity to bear in their relations with others, deal openly with conflict, work effectively in groups, and understand the importance of communication. They can now get ahead for this, not necessarily for just being independent and entrepreneurial.
>
> Before the matrix system was installed, fewer people used skills in communication and sensitivity with others, although a few of the very best leaders and motivators did. Frankly, the way to get ahead under the old system was to be an independent, hard-driving entrepreneur.

The contrast between matrix management and strictly hierarchical organizations is described by Chris Argyris, professor of organizational behavior at Harvard University:

> The pyramidal structure acquires its form from the fact that, as one goes up the administrative ladder, (1) power and control increase; (2) the availability of information increases; (3) the degree of flexibility to act increases; and (4) the scope of the decisions made and the responsibilities involved increases. Implicit in the matrix organization are almost opposite tendencies. For example, power and control are given to the individual and/or to the groups who have the technical skill to accomplish the task, no matter what their organizational level. Thus a team could be composed of five people representing all different levels

of authority (on the traditional chart), who are equal. The group
could be chaired by the individual with the least organizational
authority. The individual or groups are given responsibility and
authority to make decisions of the widest necessary scope
(including performance appraisal of that work team).[1]

Ideally, a project team works with a great deal of collaboration
and interdependence. In practice, however, many organizations
have found that without sufficient training and reinforcement team
members still tend toward competition, lack of trust, turf protection, and a desire for visible power and control—the familiar
organizational style—all to the detriment of the project. Some
organizations are seeking to remedy this by providing training in
dealing with conflict, giving support, and other interpersonal skills.
They are developing new behaviors to support the matrix system.
Clearly, if matrix management is to realize its full potential,
managers who habitually employ strictly "masculine" competencies
will need to acquire some "feminine" skills. The feminine orientation values effective two-way communication, acknowledging vulnerability, concern about relationships, and mutual support.

Managing Work and People

At this time, there are few organizations that link their assessment and hiring policies with their performance appraisal systems
and career development systems through a set of competencies that
describe an effective employee of that organization. Performance
management offers an opportunity to integrate these practices. It is
present-oriented in terms of monitoring, future-oriented in terms of
development, and past-oriented in terms of assessment.

Performance Management

Many organizations are now struggling to develop more thorough
systems of performance management. Essentially, performance

management is the process by which boss and subordinate identify and define desired work objectives, measure productivity in meeting these objectives, and plan for professional development.

Performance management is divided into five stages: (1) planning, which includes reviewing organizational goals, departmental objectives, and position descriptions in order to identify criteria for performance measurement; (2) coaching employees and measuring performance; (3) setting individual developmental plans for each employee; (4) monitoring progress; and (5) evaluating results, which involves self-appraisal and boss appraisal and the determination of pay and other personnel actions (such as rewards, citations, and promotions) on the basis of the appraisal.

Stage 1: Planning. The planning stage focuses on the identification of organizational expectations for each job in order to plan performance. Job elements are defined, including specific objectives taken from a work unit's MBO or ZBB (zero-base budgeting) plan, from the worker's job description, and from personal objectives and requirements. Problems occur at this stage if planning documents are developed without an honest interchange between workers and supervisors. To be effective, these boss-subordinate discussions should involve self-disclosure, exploration, goal setting, critical negotiation, and timely, data-based feedback. The manager needs to combine communication and goal-oriented skills to complete the planning stage of performance management.

Stage 2: Managerial coaching and measurement. The second stage involves setting specific performance goals and standards (not activities) and developing objective performance criteria for purposes of measurement. These criteria should be results-oriented, specific, clear, achievable, and challenging, and they must be backed by an action plan. The criteria should include timeliness, quality, and other characteristics of output and should differentiate between levels of performance. A performance goal can be as simple as "Revise handbook on performance appraisal by June 1" or "Set up 20 United Fund committees by October." Or it can be as complex as

"Develop subordinates in order to increase their capacity to contribute to the organization" or "Measure and improve the quality of the physical workspace."

Performance goals and measurement criteria need to be reexamined periodically to determine if the original goals remain realistic, given additional assignments and shifting priorities. Coaching by the manager along the way provides developmental feedback. The manager needs to maintain some anecdotal record so that the final appraisal can be sufficiently specific.

Craig E. Schneier, professor of management at the University of Maryland, has outlined several possible areas of measurement: quantity, quality, cost control, timeliness and dependability, training, maintenance, employee satisfaction, profit, technique, and accomplishments.[2] The following are examples of specific outcomes used as measures: transfers due to unsatisfactory performance, training programs attended, minority persons hired, items entered in a ledger, reduction in expenses from previous period, extent of contribution and amount of innovation in the project, cost of material used in training, community complaints received, grievances received, returned goods, rate at which individuals advance, transfers at employees' request, employees ready for assignment, and complaints from employees.[3]

Stage 3: Development. The third stage of performance management determines the direction of the employee's individual development plan. Deficiencies in job skills are identified and areas of growth and development are pinpointed. A careful diagnosis of ineffective performance is critical. This should be followed by the construction of an action plan to correct deficiencies, either through training programs and developmental job assignments or through enrollment in degree programs, networking, or mentoring.

Diagnosis of low performance may show that it is due to:

1. Lack of knowledge or skill, in which case training is required.
2. Personal problems or lack of motivation, in which case counseling may be relevant.

3. Lack of clear expectations, in which case managerial coaching is required.

4. Lack of sufficient resources, equipment, or funds, in which case organizational priorities need to be set.

Supervisors and workers need to communicate in a highly supportive atmosphere for maximum self-disclosure and exploration of aspirations. During this phase the supervisor is both a manager and a counselor.

Stage 4: Monitoring progress. Within four to six months maximum, the first formal review takes place. (Ideally, of course, reviewing is a continuous process.) In reviewing and monitoring, the manager probes, clarifies, coaches, and provides feedback on how well standards are being met. Or, if the nature of the employee's work has shifted, the manager negotiates new goals.

Stage 5: Evaluation and determination of rewards. In the final stage, supervisor and employee measure actual accomplishments against the original goals and performance criteria. This assessment process should be both analytical and judgmental. The goals of evaluation are (1) to reach a mutual understanding of what the employee actually accomplished by means of self-appraisal and boss appraisal; (2) to diagnose causes of low performance when it occurs; (3) to develop an action plan to improve low performance; and (4) to indicate other personnel decisions, such as a bonus or promotion or a warning about unsatisfactory performance. The relevant skills for the manager at this stage include eliciting information and probing cause and effect without making the employee feel inhibited or punished.

For both boss and subordinate, the evaluation stage calls for an atmosphere that encourages two-way communication. Employees who feel threatened or afraid to ask questions when they do not understand are likely to resist change. And employees who see evaluation as punitive will defend against it, holding back valuable information to protect themselves.

The objective at this point is to change nonproductive behavior and to help the employee increase his or her effectiveness. Under-standing at this stage is critical. Even if employees leave the organization as a result of the review process, through personal choice or management choice, they must be clear about the reasons if they are to use the information for further development and future job selection. Understanding is critical to the manager as well, in order to develop employees for future contributions to the organization.

A useful way to evaluate the appraisal process is to ask the following questions:

Were boss and subordinate realistic?

Did they have a data base for their judgments?

Were they collaborative—not forcing opinions and information on each other?

Did they alternate between talking and listening, encouraging each other to express opinions and ideas?

Did they build on each other's ideas?

Why All the Concern Over Appraisal?

Why is performance appraisal so difficult an experience? Why does so much attention have to be paid to it? What all the forms really add up to is *the conversations*. If the critical four hours of conversation a year are not open, with a free exchange of informa-tion, feelings, and judgments, then nothing has really happened. The supervisor has not functioned effectively in managing, coach-ing, and giving feedback to the employee. These conversations will run smoothly if there is agreement between the supervisor and the employee on both the quality of performance and what the reward for performance should be. However, if the supervisor's and the employee's perceptions differ, the situation may become a confron-tation. Research has shown that employees usually rate their performance higher than their supervisors do, whereas supervisors think they have the big picture in mind and that a particular employee is not a great deal stronger than any other.

It is essential that employees see the appraisal process as being closely linked to personnel actions; otherwise, the system loses meaning. The effectiveness of such a process depends on collaboration between supervisor and subordinate. Schneier notes that the major problems in performance appraisal occur because of bias and errors in human judgment, stereotypes and prejudices, and failure to use all available performance information in making ratings. Both the recency of an outstanding piece of work (the "halo" effect) and the recency of ineffective performance (the "horns" effect) can bias the rater.

Problems also occur because of difficulty in developing specific performance criteria, omission of one or more relevant aspects of job performance, and contamination of the criteria with factors that may not have an impact on job success (for example, appearance). But Schneier stresses that most appraisal systems are less than effective not because of problems with the appraisal forms but because (1) organization policy does not stress the importance of appraisal as a management responsibility; (2) there is no clear relationship between the results of appraisal and reward or promotion decisions; and (3) little attention is paid to the individual's need for feedback and development.

Many managers are extremely uncomfortable about giving negative feedback. They hold back from developing close relationships with employees just so they can offer criticism, and sometimes this makes the appraisal process all the more difficult. Earl Weaver, whom many consider to be one of baseball's best managers, holds this belief:

A manager has to stay away from his players. You have to be mature enough to realize that the day will come when you will have to look every one of them in the eye and say, "You can't cut it anymore." You're the one who has to fire them, bench them, trade them. You're the one who decides all the worst things in their lives. And you have to do that for twenty-five guys. To be fair, to keep your job, to have the best possible team, you must keep your distance, no matter how much you like the guy.[4]

Weaver states a strong desire to maintain a professional distance between himself and his players. He likes his players but does not want to care so much for them that if they stopped performing effectively he couldn't tell them so. It is a common fear that expressive "feminine" behavior leads to such overinvolvement that a person is unable to be critical. (What does this say about falling in love and deciding to get married?) Yet how long would a player perform for a manager if he felt the manager didn't like him or didn't care about him?

Weaver's actions belie his words. The fact is that Weaver does show concern for his players, primarily through the openness of his communications. He selects positions for his players on the basis of their skills, monitors their training to increase their effectiveness at the positions, and gives feedback—both negative and positive—on their performance. In other words, Weaver is effective because he is an androgynous manager: he is able to communicate openly with his players, be sensitive to their needs, develop them, and still retain his more objective "masculine" behaviors.

The fear of being controlled by personal feelings is expressed by managers in every type of organization, from the smallest nonprofit agency to the Executive Office of the President of the United States. Following his cabinet shakeup in July 1979, when he was accused of making decisions based on personalities, President Jimmy Carter ordered that the performance of the top layer of political appointees be appraised. He wanted to convey the image of a tough, take-charge manager. Instead, he appeared to strike out harshly. Carter used only one aspect of performance management—evaluation. He did not utilize the tool effectively, because he ignored the manager-subordinate discussions at the planning, monitoring, reviewing, and development stages. (See Figure 7-1.)

Carter's appraisal violated the spirit of performance management because it was a surprise attack. The evaluation did not include

Figure 7-1. President Carter's staff evaluation form.

Office:_____
Name of Rater:_____

STAFF EVALUATION

Please answer each of the following questions about this person.

Name:_____
Salary:_____
Position:_____
Duties:_____

Work Habits:

1. On the average when does this person: arrive at work _____
                                             leave work _____

2. Pace of Work: 1   2   3   4   5   6
                        slow   fast

3. Level of Effort: 1   2   3   4   5   6
                        below   full
                        capacity   capacity

4. Quality of Work: 1   2   3   4   5   6
                        poor   good

5. What is he/she best at? (rank 1-5)   ____Implementing
   ____Conceptualizing   ____Attending to detail
   ____Planning   ____Controlling quality

6. Does this person have the skills to do the job he/she was hired for?
   yes ____   no ____   ? ____

7. Would the slot filled by this person be better filled by someone else?
   yes ____   no ____   ? ____

Personal Characteristics:

8. How confident is this person? (circle one)
        x   x   x   x   x   x
        self-   confident   cocky
        doubting

9. How confident are you of this person's judgment?
        1   2   3   4   5   6
        not   very
        confident   confident

10. How mature is this person?
        1   2   3   4   5   6
        immature   mature

11. How flexible is this person?

	1	2	3	4	5	6
		rigid			flexible	

12. How stable is this person?

	1	2	3	4	5	6
		erratic			steady	

13. How frequently does this person come up with new ideas?

	1	2	3	4	5	6
		seldom			often	

14. How open is this person to new ideas?

	1	2	3	4	5	6
		closed			open	

15. How bright is this person?

	1	2	3	4	5	6
		average			very bright	

16. What are this person's special talents?

1_____

2_____

3_____

17. What is this person's range of information?

	1	2	3	4	5	6
		narrow			broad	

Interpersonal Relations:

18. How would you characterize this person's impact on other people? (for example, hostile, smooth, aggressive, charming, etc.)

1_____

2_____

3_____

19. How well does this person get along with

Superiors	1	2	3	4	5	6
Peers	1	2	3	4	5	6
Subordinates	1	2	3	4	5	6
Outsiders	1	2	3	4	5	6
	not well				very well	

20. In a public setting, how comfortable would you be having this person represent:

you or your office	1	2	3	4	5	6
the President	1	2	3	4	5	6
	uncomfortable				comfortable	

21. Rate this person's political skills.

	1	2	3	4	5	6
		naive			savvy	

Supervision and Direction:
22. To what extent is this person focused on accomplishing the

    administration's goals   ___%
    personal goals   ___%
                                    100%

23. How capable is this person at working toward implementing a decision with which he/she may not agree?
              1   2   3   4   5   6
              reluctant   eager

24. How well does this person take direction?
              1   2   3   4   5   6
              resists   readily

25. How much supervision does this person need?
              1   2   3   4   5   6
              a lot   little

26. How readily does this person offer to help out by doing that which is not a part of his/her "job"?
              1   2   3   4   5   6
              seldom   often

Summary:
27. Can this person assume more responsibility?
    yes   ___   no   ___   ?   ___

28. List this person's 3 major strengths and 3 major weaknesses.
    Strengths: 1_____
    2_____
    3_____
    Weaknesses: 1_____
    2_____
    3_____

29. List this person's 3 major accomplishments.
    1_____
    2_____
    3_____

30. List 3 things about this person that have disappointed you.
    1_____
    2_____
    3_____

CARL A. RUDISILL LIBRARY
LENOIR RHYNE COLLEGE

manager-subordinate planning. It was sent to a third party, in many cases without the subordinate ever seeing it.

Many of the questions on the evaluation form called for subjective judgments—for example, rating the quality of work from poor to good on a scale of 1 to 6 and rating staff as self-doubting, confident, or cocky. The question "Would the slot filled by this person be better filled by someone else?" is only perplexing and threatening. When there are developmental questions (for example, "What are this person's special talents?"), they are not tied to a developmental plan. The cost of utilizing appraisal strictly for evaluation is that the impact on morale of such a judgmental act can be and was in this particular case quite negative. Appraisal is a powerful management tool that must ultimately improve individual and work unit functioning if it is to be effective.

To summarize, performance management is a critical set of practices for monitoring work, planning the development of employees, and making systematic rather than capricious personnel decisions. Without a comprehensive, carefully orchestrated system of both performance management and career management, employee effectiveness and organizational effectiveness will be strongly impaired.

The success of such a system does not depend on a carefully constructed set of forms or a systematic set of practices—although these are critical. Rather, its success is contingent upon bosses and subordinates talking to each other—through the use of an androgynous blend of skills—so that feedback may be given freely and support for change can actually come about. The alternative is grim: if communication is closed, neither party will be able to hear the other and hence each will resist and subvert the other's goals.

NOTES

1. Chris Argyris, "Today's Problems with Tomorrow's Organizations," in
   Jong S. Jun and William B. Storm, eds., *Tomorrow's Organizations:
   Challenges and Strategies* (Glenview, Ill.: Scott, Foresman, 1973).
2. Stephen J. Carroll and Craig Eric Schneier, *Performance Appraisal and
   Development* (Santa Monica, Cal.: Goodyear, forthcoming).
3. Richard W. Beatty and Craig Eric Schneier, *Personnel Administration: An
   Experiential Skill-Building Approach*, 2nd ed. (Reading, Mass.: Addison-
   Wesley, 1981).
4. Earl Weaver in *The Washington Post*, April 6, 1979, p. D3.

8

Human Resources Development and Androgyny

The strategies and values most indicative of an organization that fosters androgynous behavior are those aimed specifically at developing human resources and supporting people's efforts to further personal and organizational goals. These programs tend to be growth-oriented and to encourage fuller expression on the part of employees.

Effective human resources management programs encourage employees to develop new skills; reward effective managerial behavior; offer employees meaningful, well-planned work; match people with jobs for management succession; and encourage autonomy and colleagueship in accomplishing the work.

Inadequate human resources management can have disastrous consequences for the organization. According to Lynden V. Emerson, director of the Performance Development Group at the U.S. Department of Commerce, these consequences are:

○ Potential candidates are not attracted to the organization.
○ The wrong people are selected for certain jobs.

- Money and time are wasted on the wrong training or development experiences.
- Morale is lowered when clear distinctions in performance are not made or mediocre performance is rewarded.
- Incentive is quashed when everyone receives the same wage increase or when clearly superior performers receive bonuses that are not much larger than those given to mediocre performers.
- The wrong people are identified for advancement, and management succession is poorly planned.
- Good employees become disgruntled and leave the organization because of its failure to identify potential or to accurately reward performance.
- Employees complain about and challenge management decisions through informal grievances and full-scale lawsuits.[1]

The thesis of this book, once again, is that expressive behaviors—namely, a sensitivity to personal needs and to alliance building—are just as important as task-oriented behaviors—setting high standards for oneself and others—in managing today's workforce and improving productivity. This blend of male and female qualities—androgynous behavior—is the promise of better management in the future. This chapter illustrates an androgynous approach to career management, training and development, and affirmative action.

Career Management

Career management requires the same kind of coaching and counseling skills that managers use in performance appraisal. The following mixture of androgynous characteristics is called for:

1. The manager helps to build a supportive climate in which employees identify their skills.
2. The manager acts assertively to help employees determine whether the skills they identify are in fact skills they possess.

3. The manager demonstrates understanding and patience in getting people to talk readily and positively about themselves.

4. The manager discloses information about himself or herself in order to serve as a model.

A line manager needs to know each employee's career plans in order to share in setting and evaluating goals. Beverly Kaye, an organization consultant specializing in career development in Los Angeles, describes the following stages of career management:

Preparation. Before talking with the employee, the manager assesses the employee's strengths and weaknesses, the options for career paths in and out of the organization, the resources available for development, and how the direction in which the organization is moving may affect the employee's career.

Profiling. The line manager meets with the employee to talk about the fit of values, skills, and interests with the organization and to give feedback on administrative and technical skills.

Targeting. The manager and employee work on goal setting, beginning, perhaps, with the employee listing a number of different goals. The manager can help the employee plan the steps necessary to reach his or her goals by looking at what the potential barriers are to reaching a particular goal and who else is available in the organization to encourage the employee.

Whenever necessary, the manager should share important information about the organization as a reality check. For example, a bank may be planning to eliminate tellers in five years because it will be completely automated. The manager may need to point out that there are a variety of career options for the employee and encourage the employee to develop contingency plans. These options are characterized by Beverly Kaye as:

Lateral—cross-functional movement (new way of using already developed skills).

Vertical—movement up the hierarchical ladder.

Enrichment—increased challenge in current job.

Exploratory—exploration of another job possibility while still at current job.

Realignment—downward transfer for a less stressful job or a developmental opportunity.

Relocation—movement out of the organization into another work setting.[2]

Execution. At the final stage, the manager steps back and lets the employee take some risks and execute the strategies that they planned. Here the manager works best by being supportive but not dominant, loyal but not forceful. Some employees will not make needed changes or execute their strategies. At this point, the manager will have to decide when to push and when to let go.

The manager's reward for developing employees is a more effective organization in which people are utilized productively and are ready to move into open slots without delay. The employee's reward is progress in achieving his or her goals.

Training and Development

Training and development is essentially continuing education for adults. Ideally, it serves the employee's need to increase his or her skills for present and potential jobs and the organization's need to systematically develop employees and plan for their succession. Programs to support skills development range from informal on-the-job coaching and counseling to formal off-site training; from organizational management institutes to packaged programs sponsored by training organizations. The existence of training and development opportunities identifies an organization that places high priority on human resources development. This is particularly true if the training and development opportunities are designed to reflect a clear assessment of employee needs and organizational goals and priorities.

In most organizations, however, training and development programs are ad hoc and incidental. Only rarely are they linked to thoughtful, sequential developmental plans or to assessments of personal and organizational needs. Too often, training and development course offerings are based on what is available at the local university, the latest fad, personal requests, or, especially in the case of sending people to conferences or professional meetings, who has seniority and is most deserving. This has little relationship to effective planning for human resources utilization and systematic developmental plans for each employee.

A more proactive stance for an organization is to assess the specific skills employees need and then to design and deliver programs that take into account the manager-subordinate and natural work team relationships. All this requires effective masculine instrumental behavior as well as feminine expressive behavior. The time spent in assessment is readily compensated for by eliminating the time wasted in "car wash" or "sheep dip" training programs that send everyone through the same structured experience without attention to individual skill levels.

If training and development is to benefit both work and workers, the all too frequent approach of circulating a sign-up list of courses available must be replaced. Instead, good communication and a clear set of expectations are required to help employees define and express developmental needs and to create a match between these needs, the training opportunities, and the effective accomplishment of the job itself. This is happening on a growing scale in organizations that view human resources development as an essential component of their growth and survival.

Because training needs differ with age as well as sex, assessment is especially important. To the extent that women and men were socialized differently, both are culturally deprived and can benefit from learning each other's skills. These notions offer support to single-sex training as well as mixed-group training. Organizations need to offer learning opportunities for different cultural groups, ranging from women-in-management courses, to development programs for black managers, to courses in men and women in organizations.

Coaching by supervisors on job performance is an important strategy for employee development. Here again, the traditional "feminine" skills of understanding and alliance building are particularly valuable.

An effective coach takes time out regularly to help a subordinate grow through discussions, introductions to others who can help, suggestions about educational opportunities and background reading, and entree to professional organizations. By improving employee performance and development, such efforts help shift responsibility for the work lower in the organization.

Managers shy away from coaching for many reasons—for example, "It takes too much time," "I don't want to get personally involved with my employees," or "It's difficult for me to criticize a woman." However, coaching assistance is critical to both the employee and the organization.

The following inventory of work relationships raises a number of questions concerning management responsibilities. The list encompasses areas that typically require more androgynous approaches to management. Your answers will help you identify your androgynous behavior—or lack of it. The more "yes" answers you have, the more effective your approach to building work relationships.

Manager's Inventory of Work Relationships

YES NO   I. *Team Building*

___ ___   1. Do I create opportunities to include subordinates in establishing goals, schedules, and methods for getting work done?

___ ___   2. Do I collaborate with subordinates in problem solving to the fullest extent possible rather than developing my own solutions and then announcing them?

___ ___   3. Do I encourage and reward new ideas and risk taking?

___ ___   4. Do I arrange an extended session with my work group at least twice a year for planning and team building?

YES NO

___ ___   5. Am I easily accessible in the course of a week when someone has a problem to discuss?

___ ___   6. Do I listen for feelings rather than trying to present solutions quickly?

___ ___   7. Do I have one-on-one sessions with each of my employees frequently?

___ ___   8. Do I collaborate with other managers on issues that cross organizational units?

___ ___   9. Am I able to share my personal feelings (including anger, fear, and a sense of isolation) with others?

___ ___   10. Do I encourage others to share their feelings?

II. *Performance Feedback*

___ ___   1. When someone's performance is inadequate, do I confront the situation honestly rather than trying to soften the bad news by slipping it subtly into conversation?

___ ___   2. Do I give enough verbal feedback between performance appraisals to let employees know where they stand so that there are no surprises at the formal evaluation?

___ ___   3. Do I have a lot of difficulty giving women, men, or minorities negative performance data?

___ ___   4. Would my employees say they understand clearly my assessment of them?

___ ___   5. Do I understand clearly my employees' assessment of me?

___ ___   6. Do I use performance appraisal as an opportunity for two-way communication with employees about their needs, doubts, and desires?

YES   NO

___ ___   7. Do employees feel comfortable negotiating performance questions or problems with me?

___ ___   8. Do I discuss performance problems as soon as they
arise rather than waiting to see how things will work
out?

___ ___   9. Do I let people know when I think they are doing a
good job, providing more positive feedback than
negative evaluation?

___ ___   10. Do I believe that people who are performing well
deserve praise even though they are "just doing their
job"?

___ ___   11. Do I set realistic expectations?

___ ___   12. Do I deal with problem employees by confrontation
rather than avoidance?

III. *Employee Development*

___ ___   1. Do I set career goals with each employee?

___ ___   2. Do I know something about my employees' personal
lives and its impact on their work?

___ ___   3. Do I suggest ways that employees can improve their
competencies?

___ ___   4. Do employees feel they can come to me with questions about training?

___ ___   5. Do I give praise freely and encourage employee
development?

___ ___   6. Do I try to find opportunities for employees to gain
on-the-job experience?

___ ___   7. Have I established mentoring arrangements for new
employees?

___ ___   8. Do I use periodic assessments or surveys to determine
developmental needs and desires?

YES NO

___ ___ 9. Do I go to bat within the organization for a budget for training and development?

IV. *Quality of Work Life*

___ ___ 1. Do I collect data from my employees about their attitudes toward the workplace?

___ ___ 2. Do I try to find ways to add more challenge and interest to jobs that may seem dead-end and boring?

___ ___ 3. Do I ask subordinates for their suggestions on improving productivity and morale?

___ ___ 4. Do I go to bat with my supervisor for some of the organizational changes recommended by employees?

___ ___ 5. Do I make an effort to understand behavioral concepts and research related to employee motivation?

___ ___ 6. Do I experiment with techniques to improve the quality of work life and/or employee motivation?

V. *Personal Development*

___ ___ 1. Do I let my supervisor know my own developmental needs and career plans?

___ ___ 2. Do I ask to be included in formal and informal activities that might help me grow and advance?

___ ___ 3. Do I create opportunities for visibility within the organization?

___ ___ 4. Do I promote my successes so that others will appreciate my capabilities?

___ ___ 5. Do I candidly assess my weaknesses and seek ways to improve?

___ ___ 6. Do I ask for performance feedback from others?

___ ___ 7. Do I let my supervisor know of personal pressures interfering with my job?

Organization Development

Organization development (OD) originated from the behavioral science research of the 1950s and 1960s. It has been variously described as collaborative problem solving, a strategy for planned change, organizationwide education, team development, and a program to increase organizational effectiveness. In practice, it can be and has been all these things. As Michael Beer, professor at Harvard Business School, has said, there are three key ingredients for organization development: dissatisfaction, a model for change, and a process for improvement. OD mobilizes the dissatisfaction of employees as a catalyst, builds on the model for the desired change, and then designs a process that encourages the commitment of those participating in order to make change possible. Beer describes the formula as follows:

$$d \text{ (dissatisfaction)} \times m \text{ (model)} \times p \text{ (process)} > \text{status quo}$$

OD calls for next-step thinking as well as long-range planning and encourages people to develop support systems so that they do not try to work for change alone. The system calls for collaborative data collection from people at various levels of the organization in order to increase participation in decision making and in working toward mutually arrived at goals. These goals may range from organizational design to interpersonal objectives.

Organization development techniques may include role clarification, third-party consultation, needs assessment, climate surveys, strategic planning, and team building. Such an approach is relevant to a wide variety of situations, from survey feedback to assess how effectively an organization is functioning at a given time to implementation of a new system, such as automated data processing or matrix management.

The strength of OD is that it calls for typically underused feminine behaviors as well as masculine qualities. The reduced emphasis on chains of command increases communication throughout the organization. OD may require training in teamwork and coaching, participatory problem solving, open communications, and interpersonal relationship skills within and among levels of the workforce. This means that managers must be able to admit vulnerabilities and problems. They need to learn to depend on others and to value ideas that come up from the ranks.

Richard Beckhard[3] describes the values implicit in OD as follows:

- To develop a viable system that can organize work in a variety of ways, depending on tasks.
- To make both the stable and temporary systems of the organization more effective by designing built-in mechanisms for improvement.
- To move toward high collaboration and low competition between interdependent units.
- To create conditions where conflict is brought out and managed.
- To reach a point where decisions are made on the basis of the source of information rather than on organizational role.

Perhaps the greatest value of organization development is that it opens up communication in an organization. It relies on skills of analysis, initiation, and decisiveness as well as on capacities for trust, personal feedback, mutual support, and shared problem solving—all characteristics of the androgynous manager. Its benefits come from reducing wasteful competition and turf protection and increasing both relevant information and interpersonal skills that contribute to solving problems and to implementing solutions.

Developing and Managing the New Workforce

Affirmative Action

Until recently, affirmative action and equal opportunity programs focused primarily on increasing awareness of or motivating minorities and women. They were not skill-based in terms of changing behavior. Nor were they designed to change the values and norms of organizations. Many of these programs were aimed at increasing individual knowledge of relevant laws and regulations. Some, perhaps, tried to sensitize men and women to the more subtle characteristics of discrimination. Most programs did not specifically seek to improve professional relationships in the work environment. They did not attempt team building for units that had minorities and women on their work teams, for boss/women manager duos, or for boss/minority manager teams.

Fair Is Not Equal; Equal Is Not Fair

Before organizations can become multicultural environments, bosses and subordinates need to be sensitive to the concerns of people from differing cultural backgrounds. To those who argue that they treat everyone the same, the answer is "Everyone has not always been treated the same; fair is not equal." Being a member of a particular sex or ethnic group has a cultural impact on behavior of which many of us are unaware.

Furthermore, there is the overriding difference of being raised in the majority race or sex versus being raised in the minority race or sex. In the organizational world, women have the minority experience. The minority perspective has been to scan the world and to understand or even to mimic the majority when necessary. And being a minority produces, as psychologist Gordon Allport has said, feelings of frustration, hopelessness, helplessness, rage, inadequacy, and paranoia.

Those in the minority have developed an additional set of antennae by which to decode messages. At all times, the deciphering process scans for the possible discount or putdown, the potential exclusion. The other minority perspective is to suffer guilt and anxiety over whether things are happening because of their minority status or because of their personal qualities. The cultural effect of being female, Black, Hispanic, Native American, or Asian is so pervasive that it will not be undone in our lifetime.

Building an environment suited to the needs and skills of the new workforce is a different goal from trying to socialize women and minorities into mainstream organizational norms. The total workplace population, from top management to new arrivals, needs to be involved. The appropriate question to the new workforce is "What do we need to do to make this a better work environment for you?" This puts some responsibility on the organization to change behaviors and on systems to be more receptive. Such a program requires that organizations examine the value of "feminine" as well as "masculine" behaviors and the value of minority group styles as well as the traditional organizational style. This seems particularly relevant when the organization is bringing into the workforce a segment of the population valued for its interpersonal sensitivity. Then the target population of an affirmative action program would also be white males, not just women and minorites. The need for a cross-cultural experience would be shared. Each segment of the population, including white males, needs to expand its repertoire of skills. The goal is no longer to mainstream minorities but rather to share skills, open up communication, and increase the effectiveness of management practices.

To be effective, the management development component of an affirmative action program needs to include:

1. Participation by men, women, and minorities from various levels of the organization with line managers on task forces charged with changing the organizational culture.
2. Data collection about the impact of stereotyping within the organization.
3. Mixed-group discussions on the negative impact of sex-role and race stereotypes on expectations within the organization.
4. Supervisory training in human resources management, with special focus on managing in a multicultural environment.
5. Team building boss-subordinate pairs that are mixed sexually and racially.
6. Deliberate attempts to increase the visibility of women and minorities in meetings and programs.

7. Networking among women and among minorities.*
8. Specific evaluation of a manager's effectiveness with the new
   workforce based on (a) ability to communicate expectations
   and standards; (b) willingness to be open, honest, and fair; and
   (c) ability to develop trust and confidence regardless of racial,
   sexual, and cultural differences.

Issues surrounding the new workforce overlap with issues of
androgynous competencies for managers. The androgynous manager needs effective skills in dealing with people, an empathic
understanding of the needs and perceptions of specific worker
populations, and an understanding of how environmental expectations and stereotypes affect certain groups of workers. Furthermore,
androgynous managers need to value diversity as well as similarity.
The goal is to encourage differences without jeopardizing employee
effectiveness.

NOTES

1. Lynden V. Emerson, *Evaluating Your Staff* (Washington, D.C.: National
   Association of Regional Councils, 1978).
2. Beverly Kaye, *Up Is Not the Only Way* (Englewood Cliffs, N.J.: Prentice-
   Hall, forthcoming).
3. Richard Beckhard, *Organization Development: Strategies and Models* (Reading, Mass.: Addison-Wesley, 1969).

*Aerospace Corporation has done a particularly fine job of encouraging increased
consciousness and networking among women and minorities. For example, the
corporation has supported the development of an Asian-American association, a black
caucus, an Hispanic caucus, and a women's committee. The parent organization for
these four special-interest groups is the company's affirmative action advisory
committee.

Effective Interpersonal Relationships in Organizations

Traditionally, it has been the manager's job to ensure that a work group functioned well. But in the past this has largely meant a focus on task-oriented activity. It is only recently, as we recognize the diversity of the needs of the new workforce and the importance of responding effectively to these needs, that bosses are being encouraged to show greater concern for human factors. People skills—traditionally regarded as feminine (and therefore given second-class status in many organizations)—are coming to the fore as a crucial part of managerial effectiveness.

The benefits of the most refined management systems become lost if the manager-subordinate relationship or the work team is not effective. Systems presumably employing performance appraisal, management by objectives, and zero-base budgeting have been sabotaged time and again because people in the organization do not really talk to one another about what is on their minds. In one large organization, over half of a group of senior managers indicated they spent less than half an hour a year on performance appraisal, even though the results were a central factor in promotion decisions.

To be effective as bosses or subordinates, team leaders or team members, employees need to increase their interpersonal skills. They need greater self-awareness (particularly a sense of their own power needs) as well as skill in providing open communication and candid performance feedback. They need to know how to work in groups or teams, how to encourage development among their subordinates, and how to deal effectively with authority.

The work relationship can be an intense one, particularly when issues of attraction and power are at stake. Among men, the issue may be framed as loyalty. Among men and women, it may take the form of sexual attraction. As one woman manager told me:

> I asked my boss if he felt comfortable giving me constructive criticism. He said, "I'm afraid of your anger." It attacks his sexuality. It's very important for my boss to feel that he's central to my development. He experiences my anger as a form of sexual rejection. He uses me for personal and interpersonal discussions, still not for technical discussions as much. I am afraid of the attraction. He needs me to be attracted to him— demands it, like the way he wants loyalty from the guys.

Some major corporations as well as such government organizations as the General Accounting Office and NASA are beginning to require human resources management functions from their line managers. The U.S. General Accounting Office holds managers responsible for the following four functions: (1) coaching and counseling employees to increase their effectiveness; (2) developing subordinates' careers; (3) managing subordinates' performance; and (4) dealing with problem employees. (NASA adds dealing with high-potential employees.)

Manager-Subordinate Communication

Communication is undoubtedly one of the most important management functions. It helps advance relationships as well as ideas. Henry Mintzberg says managers spend between 50 percent and 90 percent of their time in interpersonal communications.[1] They are likely to spend about 10 percent of this time communicating with their bosses, 40 percent with subordinates, and 50 percent with people outside the chain of command. To do this effectively requires a great deal of interpersonal skill and concern for relationships.

Full communication requires both instrumental and expressive behaviors, especially between boss-subordinate pairs and in group settings. Instrumental acts are aimed at accomplishing tasks. They include giving and requesting information, organizing the agenda, keeping to a time frame, and asking for opinions. Expressive acts show concern for group members, for climate setting, for including others, and for maintaining group cohesiveness. They include supporting others' opinions, encouraging people to speak, relieving tension, and serving as a model for candor and honesty. Studies show that women's comments in groups tend to be more expressive, whereas men's are usually more instrumental.

A number of filters destroy communication upward and downward. Several barriers to communication have been identified by Leslie This, a consultant at Organizational Renewal, Inc., in Washington, D.C.[2] Common barriers to downward communication include:

○ Selective or inattentive listening rather than an open, receptive posture.
○ Selective filtering of information based on the manager's perception of what employees ought and ought not to be told.
○ Adding information to the original message.
○ Personal values and biases.
○ Selective filtering of messages from above because of expectations that subordinates will overreact.
○ Personal feelings of the moment.

Common barriers to upward communication include:

○ Inability to differentiate between major and minor complaints.

- Too heavy a volume of communication.
- Disguising the message.
- Anticipating the reaction to the message.
- Hoping for the best, rather than confronting all information honestly.
- Catering to others' idiosyncracies and giving them only the information they want to hear.
- Perceiving the receiver of the information inaccurately.

The benefits of open and effective communication are great. They include the opportunity to stop responding to crises, since the necessary information for planning is available in the system; greater freedom and accuracy in making decisions; greater opportunities for creativity; more options in responding to problems; an increased knowledge about the problems that do arise.

Effective communication in boss-subordinate relationships is the responsibility of both parties. Subordinates need to be able to manage their bosses, as well as vice versa. One of the most important responsibilities of subordinates is to initiate discussions with the boss about job expectations in order to learn about the boss's goals, priorities, methodology, and standards, as well as to give the boss feedback on the effectiveness of his or her supervision.

This relationship, like all relationships, requires mutual commitment in order to work. Boss and subordinate need to challenge each other, inform each other, ask each other for feedback, give feedback, share needs, build trust, acquire self-awareness, confront each other, and back off from each other.

Below is a questionnaire developed by management consultant William J. Crockett that examines boss-subordinate relationships.

Questionnaire for Dynamic Subordinancy

Where ratings are called for, use a scale of 1 (low) to 5 (high).

1. Good, solid relationships with another require that three things exist: mutual trust, mutual support, and mutual concern.

a. I rate my relationship with my boss on each of these as follows:

_____, _____, _____.

b. The behavior I see in my boss that supports each of my ratings are such things as (list)_____
_____
_____.

c. I would rate my own ability to initiate, give, and receive trust as_____
_____
_____
_____.

d. I would rate my ability to give support to my subordinates as _____, and to my boss as _____. (Explain)_____
_____
_____.

e. The things that I do for others (especially for my boss) that demonstrate to them my genuine sense of concern are (list)_____
_____
_____
_____.

2. This is the freedom level I give myself to:

	With my boss	With my subordinates
Be wrong	_____	_____
Challenge	_____	_____
Be sad	_____	_____
Be angry	_____	_____
Be confused	_____	_____
Disagree	_____	_____
Fail	_____	_____
Be successful	_____	_____
Give feedback	_____	_____
Confront	_____	_____

    a. My reasons for these ratings are:_____

_____.

    b. My perceptions of my boss that influenced my ratings are (describe)_____

_____

_____

_____.

    c. The things I have tried to change are (describe)_____

_____

_____

_____.

    d. I (have) (have not) discussed these with my boss. (Explain)___

_____

_____

_____.

3. I would rate my boss's knowledge, understanding, and concern about my needs as:

	Knowledge	Understanding	Concern
Security	_____	_____	_____
Belonging	_____	_____	_____
Influence	_____	_____	_____
Self-esteem	_____	_____	_____

    a. I would rate my own initiative at telling my boss my needs as _____. My reason for this is_____

_____

_____

_____.

    b. Some of the day-to-day things in dealing with people on the job that keep me from getting my needs met are (describe)___

_____

_____

_____.

   c. The way I usually handle these situations is to (describe)_____
_____
_____
_____.

4. My level of dependence on my boss is:
self-esteem _____ happiness _____ security _____ future
_____ job satisfaction _____ support in disagreements_____
decisions _____ problem solving _____ staff issues _____.
   a. The reasons for my ratings are (discuss)_____
_____
_____
_____.

   b. I see my boss's behavior toward me as being (different from)
(similar to) his treatment of others. How? When?_____
_____
_____
_____
_____.

5. I consider that I am about _____ in my ability to get along
with people.
   a. Some of the things that I really do well are (list 5-10)_____
_____
_____.

   b. Some of the things I might try to improve upon are (list 5)__
_____
_____.

   c. With what kinds of people do I do the best? (Describe)_____
_____
_____.

   d. In what situations do I do the best? (Describe)_____
_____
_____
_____.

6. If I were to characterize my boss as an animal, I would call him

   a _____.

   Why?_____

   _____.

   a. What are 5 characteristics of this animal?_____

   _____

   _____.

   b. In my relationship to my boss, the animal I would call myself

   is_____.

   Why?_____

   _____.

   c. What are 5 characteristics of this animal?_____

   _____

   _____.

   d. I rate myself on both *a* and *c* above as _____, _____.

   e. I find myself having mixed feelings about my boss and
      myself. For example, on the one hand I feel_____;
      on the other hand I feel_____. (Do
      three or four of these.)

   _____

   _____

   _____.

   f. I would describe our relationship as being_____

   _____

   _____

   _____.

7. Thinking of the above data:

   a. I would describe the situation as being_____

   _____.

   b. I would give myself the following advice_____

   _____

   _____

   _____.

The following questionnaire is one that I developed to improve the quality of work relationships.

Interpersonal Relationships at Work Inventory

This inventory should be filled out separately by a boss and a subordinate or by two peers.

I. *Centrality*

1. I am important to our team because_____

2. Our work relationship is important to me because_____

3. What I contribute to your success is_____

4. I feel central to our work relationship when_____

5. I feel peripheral to our work relationship when_____

6. The way we deal with my professional development is_____

7. The way we show concern for each other's personal life is_____

8. The way we deal with conflict is_____

9. The way we have fun together at work is_____

10. The way we make work satisfying/productive for one another is_____

II. *Trust / Predictability*

1. You are predictable because_____

   _____

2. You are unpredictable because_____

   _____

3. I trust you to do/be_____

   _____

4. I do not trust you to do/be_____

   _____

5. I deal with stress by_____

   _____

6. You deal with stress by_____

   _____

III. *Power / Control*

1. My workload is controlled by_____

   _____

2. The tasks I undertake are determined by_____

   _____

3. The planning for our team is done by_____

   _____

4. Taking stock of our relationship is done by_____

   _____

5. Decisions about how much time we spend working together are
   made by_____

IV. *Expressing Feelings*

1. I feel *most* free with you to express ( ) frustration, ( ) anger,
   ( ) disagreement, ( ) feelings of failure, ( ) fear, ( ) sadness,
   ( ) feelings of success. (Rank in order.)

2. I feel *least* free with you to express ( ) frustration, ( ) anger, ( ) disagreement, ( ) feelings of failure, ( ) fear, ( ) sadness, ( ) feelings of success. (Rank in order.)

V. *Communication*

1. I feel free to talk openly to you because_____

   _____

2. You encourage me to bring good news and bad news to your attention by_____

   _____

VI. *Roles*

1. I have difficulty being assertive when you_____

   _____

2. You have difficulty being assertive when I _____

   _____

3. If I were you, I would do the following differently at work:____

   _____

4. Since I am not you, I cannot object to your_____

   _____

5. The strengths of our relationship are_____

   _____

6. The weaknesses of our relationship are_____

   _____

7. Our relationship would be more effective if you_____

   _____

8. Significant people in my life would characterize our work relationship as_____

   _____

VII. *Description*

1. A metaphor that describes our relationship is_____
   _____

   A descriptive song title is_____
   A descriptive book title is_____
   A hero or heroine from literature who describes me is_____
   _____

   A hero or heroine from literature who describes you is_____
   _____

VIII. *Action Plan*

1. If I could change one thing about our relationship, it would be
   _____

2. If I could change one thing about you it would be_____
   _____

3. If I could change one thing about myself it would be_____
   _____

Effective Managers as Group Leaders and Group Members

Today's managers must increasingly rely on groups and work teams to get the job done. Much of the work of organizations takes place in groups—task forces, study groups, work groups, management teams, committees, and so on. And much frustration accompanies work in groups. The concept of androgyny helps to shed light on the issues. Working with groups may be difficult for male managers, who have traditionally been rewarded for rationality, independence, competitiveness, a win-lose style, living by rules and procedures, and entrepreneurial skills. Working with groups may also be difficult for women managers, who have been socialized to be more reactive than proactive, to moderate or sidestep conflict rather than confront it head on, and to refrain from expressing their boundaries by saying yes when they should say no. Given these norms, it is frequently difficult to achieve collaboration and team-work in organizations.

In addition, few managers receive training in group effectiveness skills, in sharp contrast to the numerous sessions of technical training they undergo. Thus engineers who become project mana-gers quickly realize how unprepared they are to build a work group when all they can rely on is their technical background. Working with groups means dealing with all kinds of needs. Clayton Aldefer, a professor of organizational behavior at Yale University,[3] refers to these group effectiveness skills as relatedness needs:

o The need to establish supportive relationships in which people share their thoughts and feelings.
o The need to be heard and understood on significant matters and to find others who will respond to self-expression with genuine interest and concern.
o The need to be liked, to be accepted, and to belong to the group.
o The need to be confirmed by others as significant and worth-while.
o The need to maintain some degree of influence or power when trying to exert leadership.

An effective group needs to concern itself both with task accomplishment (getting on with the job) and with social, emotional, and maintenance needs. Task accomplishment includes identifying mutual concerns, analyzing the problem, evaluating proposed solu-tions, and making and implementing decisions. Social, emotional, and maintenance needs involve dealing with the feelings and interac-tions of group members—factors that affect the intensity of member participation and the level of conformity and manipulation in the group.

High-pressure organizational life makes it too easy to focus exclusively on the task at hand and to ignore the fact that the interaction of group members substantially affects the functioning of the team. For example, a group may let one or two highly verbal or dominant people determine the course of action and ignore the involvement and collaboration of all group members. Yet we know from research and experience that if people begin to feel disenfranchised, they may remain silent for a time but later sabotage group decisions through lack of commitment. Typically, groups stifle spontaneity and creativity through overly rigid procedures and rules or through too little structure, which leads people to feel that nothing has been accomplished.

If groups are to function well, managers need to remember that collaboration takes longer than unilateral decision making, requires compromise, and hampers feelings of autonomy, but it may also produce better decisions, over which group members feel greater ownership. A manager accustomed to fast-paced, high-energy situations will have to exercise patience and compassion in order to nurture the collaborative process. In addition, the manager and group members need to play participant-observer roles with respect to the process so that they can make midcourse corrections if necessary.

The following ten questions, adapted from Roy O. Resnikoff, M.D.,[4] can be helpful in assessing the functioning of a work team:

1. What is the outward appearance of the work group?

2. How well do members communicate with each other? Is communication precise and direct instead of vague? How well does the group make decisions and solve problems?

3. What repetitive, nonproductive behaviors do you notice?

4. What is the basic feeling state of the group, and who carries it?

5. Which members reinforce reluctance to act, and what are the most prevalent defenses used by group members? The most common defense tactics are for group members to distract others, project blame onto others, try to smooth things over, and overintellectualize. Virginia Satir, well-known family therapist, has called these types "distractors," "blamers," "placaters," and "rationalizers."[5]

6. What subsystems are operative in the group?

7. Who carries power in the group? The person who defines the

problem, makes the rules, and determines who is in or out of the group holds the most power. Like any other system, work groups are governed by rules, and the poorly functioning group has either overly restrictive rules or too ambiguous boundaries.

8. How mature is the group in terms of dependency versus autonomy? How differentiated are group members from each other, and what are the subgroup boundaries?

9. To what extent can group members solve problems together? Are the problem-solving methods appropriate? Is the group needy and immature, rebellious, or work-oriented?

10. What are your reactions to the work group? Would you want to be a member of it? A leader of it?

Stages in Group Development

Groups, like individuals, are not static, Predictable stages of development occur in the life of any group. These stages demonstrate clearly the range of androgynous behavior necessary for effective group functioning. William B. Eddy,[6] professor of public administration at the University of Missouri, suggests the following stages:

1. *Membership and acceptance.* Does everyone feel equally involved in the group? Issues of membership and acceptance arise early in a new group. People frequently feel threatened and concerned about inclusion and identity. They wonder, "Who am I in this group? How will I be viewed by others? How will my contributions stack up? Will I be accepted and supported by these people?"

Thus issues are raised concerning self-image, self-respect, competence, belonging, status, affiliation, and acceptable and unacceptable behavior. The group can deal with these issues effectively if time is set aside for members to get acquainted and to discuss why they are in the group. As a climate of mutuality begins to develop, the group can move on. The skills relevant to inclusion and climate setting at this stage are primarily feminine—a fact that may help us understand why so many groups in organizations devote very little attention to who is on board and who isn't.

2. *Individual and group goals.* Is the group careful to identify both individual and group goals to see if they are complimentary? The group usually begins with an official statement of purpose that may or may not coincide with its real function. While the official purpose may be more or less on the table, each member also arrives with a personal set of needs and expectations. One significant issue is whether group goals are compatible with individual goals and, if not, whether members will attempt to subvert group goals to their own ends. If individual and group goals are not reconciled, group members are likely to contest objectives and directions. The behaviors relevant at this stage are primarily masculine—direct statements and goal setting—although some feminine behavior is necessary for consensus testing and harmonizing.

3. *Communication and decision making.* Does the group obtain sufficient and relevant information for decisions? Does the group identify alternative approaches in a receptive rather than highly judgmental environment? The group often moves into communication and decision-making processes after it has identified its tasks and has begun to be productive. At this stage, questions need to be formulated, information generated, ideas tested, alternatives identified, and ways of deciding upon action agreed to. Masculine, task-oriented behaviors often predominate.

An important part of the group's development at this point is establishing an atmosphere of open communication in order to promote positive relationships among members. A healthier climate prevails when group members are able to express their feelings and ideas freely, with minimal fear of risk or ridicule.

Are members speaking out without undue guardedness and jockeying for influence? Are they listening to and responding to each other? Is the discussion staying on the topic? Does the climate support creativity and reasonable risk taking as opposed to defensiveness, playing it close to the vest, and competitiveness? The effective group leader has to pay a great deal of attention to the communications process. In effect, he or she is a role model for the process as well as a referee and a coach. If the leader says, "We need to stop and examine our feelings before we proceed because they are keeping us from hearing each other," then the group has permission to deal with feelings as well as tasks. In this case, feminine (expressive) behaviors predominate.

4. *Control and organization.* As the group works together on its tasks, issues of control and organization almost invariably arise. At this stage differences must be resolved and the work coordinated so that people move in the same general direction. Is the group organized around a particular leader, task, or structure? Is it organized around members' needs? Is leadership vested in one person or is it shared? Members' reactions to the leadership and control systems are crucial. Is the leader dependable, honest, compassionate, consistent, competent, and emotionally responsive? Do group members accept and adhere to controls? Or do they resent them, avoid them when possible, and always strive to change them?

Groups that successfully resolve the issues at each of these four stages can operate more effectively, because much less energy needs to be expended in coping with problems. When the various process issues are resolved, some groups also move on to the question of how close and personal to be with each other.

Effective group work, like so much of management, places a premium on an androgynous mix of skills. As Professor Eddy notes:

Traditional male traits of task focus, objectivity, confrontation, and control are clearly important in many situations. Without them, as some free-floating counterculture groups found out in the 1960s, you have disorganization, wasted motion, and anarchy. But to build and lead groups that attain effectiveness and viability by fully utilizing their human resources, you also need some of the traits traditionally thought of as female. Sensitivity to feelings, development of support and trust, and collaboration rather than competition are important aspects of long-term group effectiveness.

It is not surprising, when you think about it, why an androgynous combination of skills is best. Much of our work with
groups of male managers involves helping them get in touch
with important aspects of the group which are normally lost
from their view—the expression of their own and others'
feelings, the need for positive and supportive interaction, and
the hazards of overuse of logical-rational modes. With women,
in contrast, our work involves encouraging directness, dealing
openly with power issues, and being clear about their boundaries. The basic point is, of course, that the full range of human
characteristics is present in groups at all times. It's just a
question of whether we decide to understand and deal with
them.

As the interpersonal side of management continues to gain in
importance, androgynous behavior will become all the more valuable. Today, more and more of the manager's time is spent working
collaboratively. The manager needs to conduct career development
sessions and performance appraisals, run productive meetings,
develop short-range and long-range plans in groups, lead task forces
and study groups, and build open communications to improve the
quality of work. Thus an androgynous blend of skills—of task-
focused and people-focused behavior—is no longer a luxury but a
crucial part of managerial effectiveness.

NOTES

1. Henry Mintzberg, *The Nature of Managerial Work* (New York: Harper &
   Row, 1973).
2. Leslie This, *Guide to Effective Management* (Reading, Mass.: Addison-
   Wesley, 1974).
3. Clayton Aldefer, *Existence, Relatedness, and Growth: Human Needs in
   Organizational Settings* (New York: Free Press, 1972).
4. Adapted from Roy O. Resnikoff, "Teaching Family Therapy: Ten Key
   Questions for Understanding the Family as Patient." Unpublished
   manuscript, 1979.

5. Virginia Satir, *Peoplemaking* (Palo Alto, Cal.: Science and Behavior Books, 1975).
6. William B. Eddy, "The Manager and the Working Group." Unpublished manuscript, 1980, School of Public Administration, University of Missouri, Kansas City (copyright by the author).

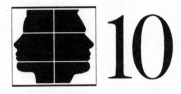

10

Androgyny
as an Antidote
to Stress

Male managers and now more and more women managers often pay a high price for the way they lead their lives in organizations. While the rewards may seem compelling in terms of prestige, accomplishment, and financial success, the penalties can be even higher. They include anxiety, stress, and such physical breakdowns as heart disease, hypertension, gastrointestinal problems, and stroke. The impact of too much stress presents one of the strongest arguments for androgyny—for merging feminine and masculine behaviors. Stress can be released when we express our feelings rather than suppress them and let go occasionally rather than continually hold on.

Effective stress management ultimately requires changing the way we cope with pressure and crisis. As John Adams, an organization and stress consultant in Washington, D.C., says:

People need to assume personal responsibility for their own

well-being. It is not enough to say, "I'd like to change, but the organization requires that I keep driving myself." Unless one takes responsibility, one stays the "victim" who can't change. Each person must make the choice for a less stressful approach to life and work. If the person is self-responsible, then he or she will or won't change, but outside factors cannot be held responsible.[1]

To manage stress in a responsible way, both sexes need to give up the extremes of their behavior. For men, this means easing up on strict emotional control. For women, it means abandoning such "feminine" behaviors as dependency, waiting for others' advice, and allowing others to plan their activities. For both sexes, a state of well-being can be attained by introducing more balance into life—in work and play, friendship and fun, self-control and self-indulgence, solitude and love. This chapter outlines several sources of organizational, environmental, and personal stress and shows how androgyny can be an effective antidote to present hard-driving lifestyles.

Causes of Stress

For both men and women, stress is due in part to the nature of the organization and the climate in which work is done. Stressful work climates—those that are toxic to the individual—include a high degree of evaluation and control, an emphasis on one-up/one-down relationships, and an unnecessarily high value being placed on the right answer. Many of these characteristics are deeply ingrained in our technocracy.

Some of the factors that produce particularly high stress are described by Michael T. Matteson and John M. Ivancevich:[2]

Personal Stressors

1. Work quantity that exceeds expectations or is cyclical in nature so that there are high stress periods.

2. Responsibilities for others' careers and welfare that become overly burdensome.
3. Work difficulty that exceeds expectations.
4. Role ambiguity resulting from lack of clear feedback or clear lines of responsibility.
5. Role conflicts that place the manager in the middle, forcing him or her to wear several different hats—for example, those of administrator, faculty member, and consultant.
6. Frustration with rate of career progress or dissatisfaction with status in the organization.
7. Rapid or unexpected rate of change, such as during a reorganization.
8. Lack of group cohesiveness.
9. Intragroup conflict.
10. Group dissatisfaction.

Organizational Stressors

11. Organizational climate, such as heavy time pressures and few rewards.
12. Inadequate or new technology.
13. Management styles, such as firefighting rather than planning or constantly shifting priorities.
14. Control systems, such as a transfer against will.
15. Organizational design, such as unclear authority structure.
16. Job design, such as routinized work or dead-end position.
17. Job characteristics.

Extraorganizational Stressors

18. Family problems, such as serious illness, divorce, death, moving, children leaving home, parents suffering old-age problems.
19. Economic problems.
20. Political uncertainty, such as imminent change in administration.
21. Lack of mobility.

Men and Stress: The Type A Personality

Ray Rosenman and Meyer Friedman, studying 3,500 men in a long-term analysis of life patterns and health, found that those who exhibited Type A behavior were three times more likely to break down than those who exhibited Type B.[3] The Type A pattern is characterized by an unemotional, single-minded pursuit of a goal, a chronic sense of urgency, a drive for achievement, and a competitive approach to most tasks. Since this style is often associated with managerial success, women moving into the ranks of managers are adopting it as well as men and then suffering from the consequences.

Type A people are constantly on guard. They are unable to relax or depend on others, so they rely only on themselves. They constantly work against time and are always on the go. They begin

I Have Arrived
Natasha Josefowitz

I have not seen the plays in town
   only the computer printouts
I have not read the latest books
   only *The Wall Street Journal*
I have not heard birds sing this year
   only the sound of typewriters
I have not taken a walk anywhere
   but from the parking lot to my office
I have not shared a feeling in years
   but my thoughts are known to all
I have not shed a tear in ages
   but when I shout they tremble
I have not listened to my own needs
   but what I want I get
I have arrived—
   is *this* where I was going?

thinking about one activity before another is finished. Type A's sometimes complete others' sentences, have difficulty waiting in line, and have scheduling problems because they are trying to crowd so much in.

Type A's exhibit tough-cool, superhuman behavior. They cannot admit vulnerability to others; and they so dislike warm or helpless feelings in themselves that they often deny they exist. Because Type A's have difficulty maintaining close relationships, they usually lack support systems and feel they must be the only ones to do the job. By ignoring nonverbal behavior, they tend to miss a lot of the context of communication.

Type A's typically ignore their own psychological needs. They do not manage their aggressive feelings and hence express high power needs, almost to the exclusion of needs for affiliation. They have difficulty controlling impulses and are egotistic, generally orienting conversations to their own concerns. They are impatient with others' needs or points of view and tend to ignore the importance of other people's values. For instance, Type A's may not deal with conflicts stemming from differing priorities about work and family life. They typically evaluate in terms of quantity rather than quality— bigger is better. With their excessive focus on task, they cannot observe well. They lack awareness of the positive or negative aspects of their physical surroundings.

Peter Sacks, head of the Division of Preventive Medicine at the Scripps Clinic Medical Group, Inc., in La Jolla, California, does screening for various corporate executives. He says:

> Type A behavior is often complicated by restless sleep resulting
> in chronic fatigue, mild depression, and loss of interest in sex.
> Further symptoms that may occur in some include headache,
> dizziness, and tension in the neck and upper back muscles, as
> well as colonic spasm with abdominal discomfort. These are
> usually manifestations of decompensation in a stressed Type A
> individual. Sexual intercourse, under these circumstances, is
> often used as a "release" from tension rather than as a sponta-
> neous or intimate response to another individual.

Finally, Type A people avoid or are reluctant to express "feminine" behaviors. For example, they feel uncomfortable crying, or even saying they feel like crying, or expressing other tender feelings. It would disrupt their work style, which is smooth, rational, analytical, and oriented toward problem solving.

Because Type A personalities are so vulnerable to the ill effects of stress, it is important to know your personality style. Are you Type A or Type B? The following questionnaire can help you "type" your behavior.

Type Your Behavior*

Directions: To obtain an estimate of your behavior type, answer the following questions by indicating the response that *most often* applies to you:

YES   NO

___ ___ 1. When you are under pressure or stress, do you usually do something about it immediately?

___ ___ 2. Has your spouse or friend ever told you that you eat too fast?

___ ___ 3. When people take too long to come to the point in a conversation, do you often "put words in their mouth" in order to speed things up?

___ ___ 4. Do you often find yourself doing more than one thing at a time, such as working while eating, reading while dressing, or figuring out problems while driving?

___ ___ 5. Do you feel irritated if someone interrupts you while you are in the middle of something important?

___ ___ 6. Are you always on time, or a little bit early for appointments?

*From Meyer Friedman and Ray H. Rosenman, *Type A Behavior and Your Heart* (New York: Random House, 1974). Adapted by permission.

YES NO

__ __ 7. Do you feel impatient or restless when forced to "wait in line," such as at a restaurant, store, or post office?

__ __ 8. Do you find competition on the job or in outside activities enjoyable and stimulating?

__ __ 9. Nowadays, do you consider yourself to be definitely hard-driving and competitive?

__ __ 10. Would people who know you well rate your general level of activity as "too active" and advise you to "slow down"?

__ __ 11. Would people who know you well agree that you tend to get irritated easily?

__ __ 12. Would people who know you well agree that you tend to do most things in a hurry?

__ __ 13. Would people who know you well agree that you have more energy than most people?

__ __ 14. Do you enjoy competition and try hard to win?

__ __ 15. Is it very difficult for you to relax after a hard day?

__ __ 16. In your opinion, do top executives usually reach their high positions through hard work rather than social skills and the luck of "being in the right place at the right time"?

__ __ 17. During the average busy workweek, do you usually spend more than 50 hours working?

__ __ 18. Do you usually go to your place of work when you are not expected to be there (for example, weekends) at least once a week?

__ __ 19. Do you bring work home or study work-related materials more than once a week?

__ __ 20. Do you often stay up later than you prefer or get up early in order to get more work done?

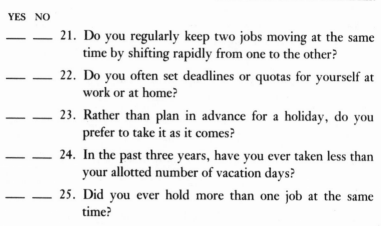

YES   NO

___ ___ 21. Do you regularly keep two jobs moving at the same time by shifting rapidly from one to the other?

___ ___ 22. Do you often set deadlines or quotas for yourself at work or at home?

___ ___ 23. Rather than plan in advance for a holiday, do you prefer to take it as it comes?

___ ___ 24. In the past three years, have you ever taken less than your allotted number of vacation days?

___ ___ 25. Did you ever hold more than one job at the same time?

Type A behavior can be determined accurately only by a structured interview. However, if you have answered yes to more than 15 of these questions, you are more than likely a Type A person.

Type A people are aggressively involved in an incessant struggle to achieve more and more in less and less time and, if required, to do so against the opposing efforts of other things or other people. A new challenge always serves as a fuse for an explosion of Type A behavior.

Type B people are less harried by desires to obtain a steadily increasing number of things or participate in an endlessly growing series of events in an ever decreasing amount of time. They have a greater sense of balance about their lives. They can find fun and relaxation in play rather than using it to demonstrate superiority. They can work without agitation and relax without guilt.

Women and Stress: Culture Shock

Women in organizations frequently experience stress from culture shock. Entry into the white male system often conflicts with traditional female values, self-perceptions, and expectations about life and work. When a woman becomes a manager, she must deal with (1) high visibility and accompanying social pressure; (2) exclusion from the informal communications network; (3) competition with other women; (4) relative powerlessness and lack of experience in the use of power; and (5) anger, which the system defines as irrational and inappropriate. If she has trouble adjusting, all too often the system conveys to the confused woman the message that there is something wrong with her. This message is easily believed. As a result, she views the problem as hers, and her solution is to try to change herself. The system is not questioned. In this way, the woman chooses to be the victim of the situation rather than challenging the system's values.

These adjustment problems cause intense stress and a host of negative feelings for women. Linda Moore, an organization consultant and therapist in Kansas City, describes the syndrome:

> Since the system typically discourages open expression of feelings, many women store up this "emotional garbage" as if their bodies were trash compactors. In effect, women emulate their male counterparts. In doing so, they become more vulnerable to so-called male diseases, such as coronary artery disease. The internal pressure of the unexpressed emotions builds up, layer after layer, until coping with the stress feels impossible.

The result: angry, emotional outbursts; a tendency to cry easily; physical symptoms such as dizziness and indigestion; and physical illness. The system regards all these responses as inappropriate. So the woman-as-victim cycle continues. To break the cycle, women need to understand how the system and its traditional white male values contribute to the problems and why stress results.

The Impact of Stress

A wide range of individual differences contribute to how stress affects people and how they respond to it. These include differences in ambitiousness, degree of drive, sense of urgency, rational and objective thinking, organizational skills, number of hours worked, tolerance for ambiguity, degree of control over feelings and emotions, tendency to feel pressured, fear of failure, and willingness to make sacrifices for career success. Physical and emotional factors include heredity, age, sex, alcohol and tobacco use, amount of exercise, family medical history, amount of support, and basic health.

The symptoms of stress are evident in breakdowns in the functioning of the body, in increased psychological anxiety, and in reduced productivity at work. Physiological symptoms known to be related to stress include hypertension, ulcers, tension in the back, and migraines. Psychological manifestations include obsessive worrying, hostile outbreaks, bitchiness, fatigue, sleep problems, smoking, drinking, depression, changes of interest in sex and eating, thoughts about suicide, disorientation, and generally feeling unhealthy.

Not only individual costs but organizational costs are high. For instance, most heart attack victims are 45 to 65 years old, the age of executives who are usually in a position to repay the organization by providing leadership and developing subordinates. Other organizational costs include reduced performance, absenteeism, erratic productivity, and an inability to stay with a job. These symptoms can become contagious when stress gets high in a work setting, according to Dr. Michael Smith, chief of motivation and stress research at the National Institute for Occupational Safety and Health in Cincinnati. Some research and development organizations are so competitive that there is little creative research. A study of 1,200 scientists emphasized that two ingredients that ensure a constructive, productive research and development environment are a high concern for autonomy and a high concern for collaboration. Without the collaboration, ideas stagnate and people spin their wheels.

Toward a Strategy for Change

There is no question that stress in both our personal and organizational lives extracts a high cost. Is there an option? Androgyny offers an alternative to the "can-do," "tough-it-out," "what-me-vulnerable" style. In emphasizing the value of feelings and personal desires as well as achievement and action, androgyny argues against letting work take precedence over family and individual needs. It argues against taking on more and more responsibility when that is the last thing you want or need to do. It argues against repressing feelings of need or vulnerability. Stressful behavior is not only a poor managerial role model for others; it is ultimately self-destructive.

As Ray Romine, organization consultant on stress in Bellingham, Washington, says:

> The effective management of one's "stress threshold" is essential in the management of individual and organizational health. The individual who chooses to ignore the impact of physical and psychological stressors on his or her well-being by definition chooses disease over health. We are indeed responsible for the maintenance of our mind/body/spirit in living a graceful, productive life.

Exercise, meditation, and sound nutrition are all critical to stress control. Many experts in the field recommend 20 minutes a day of stretching and active breathing and at least 4 hours of exercise a week. They also encourage eating nutritious foods and cutting back on such stimulants and detrimental substances as coffee, tea, alcohol, sugar, saturated fats, salt, and chemical additives. In addition, they suggest that we monitor our own stress levels (perhaps using biofeedback), learn relaxation and meditation techniques, and develop support systems.

Time management, too, is part of stress control. As some time management courses now teach, calendars should be written in pencil so changes can be made easily. If possible, 24 hours should be allowed to weigh the pros and cons before saying yes to major commitments, and conflicts should be expressed out loud before commitments are made.

Stress control programs in organizations are aimed at (1) restructuring the work environment to make it less stressful; (2) providing management support and accountability for planning among supervisors and subordinates; and (3) finding ways to alleviate stress from cyclical work and environmental or interpersonal pressures. Organizational practices need to be redesigned to create a psychologically healthy climate as well as a physically safe one. In *Stress and the Manager: Making It Work for You*, Karl Albrecht, a consultant in San Diego, writes that we need to shift our concern from "what's good for the company is good for everybody" to "what's good for everybody is good for the company."[4]

Stress reduction facilities are being offered by a number of organizations, including Exxon, which has a physical fitness laboratory in Houston; the Pentagon, which has a meditation room as well as extensive exercise facilities; Boeing Corporation in Seattle, which turned underground tunnels into jogging tracks; 15 companies in Milwaukee that pay for programs for employees at the YMCA; and Connecticut General and Metropolitan Life Insurance companies, which have fitness facilities for employees. At Xerox Corporation, families as well as employees may use stress reduction facilities. Cummins Engine has a preventive health program in Columbus, Indiana (Columbus Occupational Health Association).

Yet exercise is only one of the facets of our lives over which we must now take control. Our entire lifestyle is being called into question because of the ever increasing demands we face in our work and home lives. For so many of us, our personal identity merges with and is absorbed by our work identity. It takes enormous self-control to extricate ourselves from organizational demands and rewards and to hold out for a balanced life of meaningful work, active involvement with others, full self-expression, and a blend of autonomy and intimacy. The goal of androgyny is to put us in touch with the full array of our feelings and needs and to help us dare to demand the right to have them met.

NOTES

1. John Adams, *Understanding and Managing Stress: A Book of Readings* (1980), University Associates, Inc., 8517 Production Road, San Diego, Cal. 92126.
2. Michael T. Matteson and John M. Ivancevich, "Organizational Stressors and Heart Disease: A Research Model," *Academy of Management Review*, Vol. 4, No. 3 (1979).
3. Meyer Friedman and Ray H. Rosenman, *Type A Behavior and Your Heart* (New York: Random House, 1974).
4. Karl Albrecht, *Stress and the Manager: Making It Work for You* (Englewood Cliffs, N.J.: Prentice-Hall, 1979).

11

Androgyny and Adult Development

Ted Kramer need not have been fired when he took over sole parenting of his son in the movie *Kramer vs. Kramer*. If his boss had acknowledged Kramer's transition, they might have been able to accommodate each other. In striking contrast is the reaction of a supervisor in a large organization to a manager whose home life was up in the air. The supervisor encouraged the manager to write into his MBO plan an objective of trying to resolve some of his personal problems in six months. And the manager could use work time to do so, provided he met his other work objectives.

People engaged in human resources planning, at both the individual and the organizational level, are becoming increasingly aware that adults do not respond to opportunities for advancement or mobility or job shifts in the same way across the board. As they probe further, researchers find that a critical factor in the choice is the point in the individual's own life when the offer of change comes. Adults are at different stages in their life cycles with respect to a job, or to the hope or despair they feel about the realization of

153

their dreams. Some organizations have dealt with the increasing barrage of information on adult transitions (midlife crises, divorce, joint custody of children, widowhood) by ignoring it; others by setting up special counseling centers; and still others by encouraging managers to become involved with employees during transitions.

The new field of adult development is growing in importance. As Zandy Leibowitz, director of career development at NASA's Goddard Space Flight Center, says:

> Adult development focuses on the identification of issues and events that adults face through the life cycle as well as on the coping strategies they employ. Adult development and career development have begun to merge in an effort to help adults plan their careers while they take into account their life stage, their career stage, and their family stage.

Today, work has become of such supreme importance to people's personal identities that it is out of balance with other aspects of their lives. Those whose identities are not confirmed through work tend to feel useless and constrained, and are easily discouraged. A survey by the American Management Associations showed that the foremost concern of middle managers was their lack of career options.[1] They felt boxed in, with limited chances for promotion. Overspecialization, they felt, was the culprit. Organizations need to take a proactive stance with respect to such concerns.

This chapter offers a look at the new field of adult development through descriptions of several of the models of adult developmental stages. In addition, it looks at the implications of the field for men's and women's lives and for the concept of androgyny.

Adult Development Theories

Until recently, efforts to study individual development began and ended with Erik Erikson's work on childhood and adolescence.

Now, with the increasing interest in adult development, a number of writer-researchers have studied adults—primarily males. What emerges is that there are a series of life tasks that all of us confront, master, adapt to, or are done in by. We define ourselves through such tasks, thereby creating a work ego, a personal identity, and intimate relationships. The ease or rigidity with which we make the transitions to the different stages says a lot about the state of our mental and physical health.

George Vaillant, M.D., of the Study of Adult Development at the Harvard University Medical School, looked at mature and immature adaptive styles, evaluating overall career, social, psychological, and medical adjustment.[2] *Career* adjustment involves the extent to which the job meets the person's needs and whether there are other outlets for using skills, such as "active public service outside the job." How the person deals with unstructured time is more important than ever to maintaining a balance between working and living, and eventually to being able to cope with retirement.

Social adjustment includes closeness—whether there is a "rich friendship pattern or a barren friendship pattern"—and styles of resolving disagreements. Vaillant defines a healthy marriage as encompassing the joyful expression of anger and sex.

Psychological adjustment includes the sense of exuberance and energy the person feels about his or her life and the degree of balance between structure and freedom. More concretely, it may be manifested by the ability to take a full vacation or to be aggressive with others. *Medical* adjustment questions include the amount of sick time per year (usually no more than five days), the use of medicines and alcohol, and the level of fatigue.

During adulthood, a healthy person evolves from being a carbon copy of parental definitions of success to becoming the architect of his or her own life. Psychologist Abraham Maslow said self-actualization does not really take place until we are 50.[3] It is not until then that many of us are able to begin living our lives according to our own desires and attitudes. Some married couples say they do not

develop their own rituals for the holidays and style at the dinner
table until long after they have been married. Until then, they try to
live up to (or rebel against) parental prescriptions.

Currently, work seems to be the primary source of self-fulfillment and self-development for men, although women appear to be
catching the disease as well. Many of the questions about values and
priorities come to the fore for men around age 40—the midlife
decade. According to Daniel Levinson, this may be a time "when
work loses its illusory magical protective powers and when we are
more in tune with our instincts and impulses. There is somehow a
reckoning with time, and a reassessment of priorities for the second
half of our lives. We may strive more for authenticity, turning to our
inner selves and becoming more reflective."[4] But there are counter-
forces, too, that are thrusting reflection and leisure upon us before
the midlife decade. These include the increasing competition for
meaningful work, alternative work patterns, shorter workweeks,
and sabbaticals. Thus we can no longer avoid confronting our
atrophied abilities to play, our desire for more joy in our lives, our
unfulfilling relationships, our aloneness and loneliness, and our
discarded dreams.

As more and more women participate in managerial work, their
adult development begins to parallel that of men. Previously,
women's lives had more transitions and more contingencies. Women
shifted from school to job to childrearing, back to school, back to
work, then to empty nest. Their decision making was based on the
course of their husband's and children's lives. They settled geo-
graphically wherever their husband's careers took them.

As mothers and daughters are finding in this time of enormous
upheaval, the rewards are quite different for the different genera-
tions. The options for many of our mothers were limited to rewards
for becoming a good wife and hostess, making an attractive nest,
caring for children, and building a social life for the family. Now the
rewards are finding significant work and a meaningful personal
identity. While women today may do some of the same activities

their mothers did—go to school, have a baby, work, have a career, get married, get divorced, get remarried—the order varies much more from person to person. The chronology is scrambled.[5] There are more choices—and more ambivalence—for women today regarding the kind of home life they want and when or if it should include children.

For both men and women, living with less structure, or more time for relationships and more time for play, calls for androgynous behavior. Many people use up a vacation by building a deck or cleaning out the attic—so-called productive activity. Often the reason is that if they had more time on their hands, they might have to confront themselves, their marriages, and their friendships with questions about authenticity and meaningfulness. Certainly in retirement, the skills for building here-and-now relationships, unhampered by shared history and unfulfilled dreams, are critical. Few people want to hear about past battles fought by retired generals while they are on the golf course. Nor do they want to walk in the woods to hear how let down parents feel by their children's inattentiveness. While grandchildren enjoy some reminiscing, how much more exciting it would be to have here-and-now spontaneity in grandparent-grandchild relationships.

Roger Gould, a psychoanalyst and professor at UCLA, sees adult life as a series of transformations during which we "reformulate our self-definition." This "dangerous act" requires us to examine truths we have clung to since childhood.[6] Such truths include:

"I'll always belong to my parents and believe in their world."

"If I get any more independent, it will be a disaster."

"My loved ones (spouse, children) can do for me what I haven't been able to do for myself."

"Doing things my parents' way, with willpower and perseverance, will bring results. But if I become too frustrated, confused, or tired, or am simply unable to cope, they will step in and show me the right way."

"Life is controllable. There are no significant coexisting contradictory forces within me."

To move unthinkingly through adult roles as if these propositions were true, as if by just clinging to them we would have a road map for life, leads to frustration and disappointment. As events unwind before us, we must take hold and build our own beliefs, or else we will need more and more props to keep us together. In all the psychological research—and in all the great novels—no one has reported fulfillment and serenity from living out someone else's script.

Androgyny and Adult Development

The concept of androgyny sums up the two central themes in adult development: autonomy and intimacy. Yet the implications of these issues for men and women are vastly different. Today many men are becoming concerned with intimacy and friendship—the feminine side—particularly with becoming closer to other men. Many women are intent on learning about their own strengths and on becoming more independent—the masculine side—as well as on building collaborative relationships with other women. This frequently means that the energy of women and men is going in different directions, and they miss each other. Both men and women must learn to appreciate each other's efforts at growth. During this period of change and transition, their identities may be quite fragile, shielded by some form of armor—be it toughness, intellectualization, withdrawal, or humor.

Why is there such a focus today on male-female relationships? Haven't men and women been marrying each other and spending their lives together for a long time? They have, but they have been struggling with the issues of autonomy, dependency, and intimacy in an intense manner for a long time too.

In her column in the local San Diego newspaper, Louise de

Graves described poignantly a typical male-female standoff in her relationship with her husband:

> Probably we married each other for all the wrong reasons. At the time, I was attracted to Ralph for his cool composure under pressure and his forcefulness, not to mention a myriad of other talents. He said he was initially attracted to me for my warmth and vulnerability. Describing these same characteristics at our second wedding anniversary, I think I called Ralph "cold and controlling" and he called me "neurotic." So much for the wisdom of mate selection.

> I have also heard it said that if people stay married, it is for different reasons than they originally married one another. This I would definitely say is true. Ralph and I have long agreed that he's had enough of my vulnerability and I've had enough of his forcefulness to last a lifetime.

Why don't these relationships work more naturally? Why are power, competition, spite, withholding, mistrust, and exploitation part of relationships? One thesis advanced by Joseph Pleck is that most men grew up in a world in which women were the primary authority figures for at least the first ten years of their lives, either as their mothers or as elementary school teachers. Many of these women were perceived at some time as extremely dominating and controlling. In addition, they were seen as the primary source of nurturance and expressiveness.[7]

For a young boy who wants warmth, compassion, and encouragement, women are both prized and feared. As boys grow up and wrestle with the world of male competition, women continue to be coveted. According to Pleck, in men's competitive struggle with other men, women are used to symbolize success, to play a mediating role between men, to offer a refuge from the stresses of the male competitive world, or to serve as the expressive partner in the male-female relationship. Women do have the power to express feelings, and men go to women to experience this kind of power.

The expectation that women will be expressive and nurturing or a refuge doesn't allow a woman much room to have her own frustrations or to satisfy her own need for space. When she is not expressive, she is seen as withholding, cold, or bitchy, rather than as human.

And so, too, men have been stereotyped. Because women were encouraged to be expressive rather than instrumental, they came to rely on men to be decisive and to take initiative, risks, and action. Since women did not have to learn to cope with the same responsibilities, they became more dependent and helpless because they lacked certain skills. Many women had absentee fathers who were workaholics and mothers who alternated between protecting the father's need to work and begrudging the less stimulating home responsibilities with which they were left. For many women, men became the coveted voice of approval, although women had to work hard for the smallest dose. Many women became competitive with their mothers for their father's approval and often felt that their mothers had nothing to offer as role models. But the mothers were not necessarily to blame. Unfulfilled and conflicted, they may not have been in a solid position to help their daughters or to be open about their own frustrations.

A lot has changed. The women's consciousness-raising and support groups of the 1970s have given way to the professional networks of the 1980s, where resources are shared, often quite eagerly, among women. Some men are opening up their relationships with other men as well, asking: "How can we be closer? How can we be less competitive?" Some women and men are talking about mutuality as the heart of a relationship, but also about how contracting and negotiation are essential parts of sharing each other's lives.

Yet so much remains to unlearn and relearn for women and men, men and other men, women and other women, in order to have adult-adult relationships in which both sides can be autonomous and intimate, supportive and separate, competent and dependent.

Survival through these changes requires a lot of support in order to hold out against rigidity. If people are to open themselves up to changes in the environment—to learn new skills rather than being limited by sex-role, age-role, or race-role expectations—we need a growth orientation, the ability to learn, and the ability to achieve balance. We must be in touch with our experiences in order to reflect, generate models, take initiative, and engage in an inner dialogue with ourselves and an open dialogue with our support systems about our goals. In addition, we need all the encouragement we can get from bosses, subordinates, spouses, children, and parents.

NOTES

1. E. Kay, *The Crisis in Middle Management* (New York: AMACOM, 1974).
2. George E. Vaillant, *Adaptation to Life: How the Best and the Brightest Come of Age* (Boston: Little, Brown, 1977).
3. Abraham H. Maslow, *Toward a Psychology of Being* (Princeton, N.J.: D. Van Nostrand, 1962).
4. Daniel J. Levinson *et al.*, *The Seasons of a Man's Life* (New York: Knopf, 1978).
5. Nancy Schlossberg and Zandy Leibowitz, *Perspectives in Counseling Adults* (Monterey, Cal.: Brooks/Cole, 1978).
6. Roger L. Gould, *Transformations* (New York: Simon & Schuster, 1978).
7. Joseph H. Pleck, "Men's Power with Women, Other Men, and Society," in Joseph Pleck and Elizabeth Pleck, *The American Male* (Englewood Cliffs, N.J.: Prentice-Hall, 1980).

12

Barriers to Interaction in Organizations

As management norms and expectations change, workers are often thrown together in situations where traditional behavioral norms are suddenly up for negotiation. The conventions of interaction in the larger society produce barriers in organizations. For men and women building adult man-woman relationships, androgyny offers a different set of norms and values.

What additional skills, behaviors, and attitudes are necessary to succeed in the new organizational environment? When women and men interact on the job, how do stereotypes get changed? Or how do people react to yelling, crying, and other expressions of hurt or anger suddenly heard in the workplace for the first time? How does a black person behave in a world of multiple expectations? He or she may face unspoken demands to act like the stereotypical black male or female, an androgynous paragon, and a white male manager—all at the same time.

This chapter examines in greater depth the results of my survey of line managers and management consultants and the in-depth interviews with two white women managers, Ellen Howe and Carol Gibson, and two black managers, Buford Macklin and Elsie Cross.

On Being Black and a Manager

Conflicting expectations make it very difficult for a black man to express androgynous behaviors, according to Buford Macklin, a black government supergrade manager:

> If you're conciliatory and try to fit in, then you're homogenized and invisible. Your energy must go to convincing people you're competent. It's never a given, but instead, time and again, it's an uphill battle to prove competence. It's like you're incompetent until you prove otherwise. This means you must be focused and single-minded in your actions. The qualities of androgyny detract from this.

For example, Macklin said, disclosing personal feelings did little to help him climb the management ladder. "It's construed as being soft, indecisive, and unclear. It just does not score the right kind of points to share personal data in the organization with my boss, subordinates, or even colleagues."

To Macklin, style is important. "Credibility requires you to have a strong rational style." But if style clashes with image, colleagues may be taken aback. Macklin offered this example:

> When I started wearing a beard, which some saw as a militant appearance, and I continued to act like the rational problem solver I am, many people seemed to be surprised and uncomfortable with me. They expected me to be aggressive. I know that the people I've had problems relating to thought that when I was a rational, logical, problem solver, I was weak and, worse, that I was being devious and insincere because my image and behavior were different. Yet, in actuality, I am much more

comfortable with a logical-thinker style, particularly given my previous training as a scientist.

So, even when displaying behaviors that were valued in management circles, Macklin was seen as weak and insincere. He equated androgyny for a black male with being invisible and giving up the struggle for advancement. "People may feel safe with you," he said, "but the black person won't get anywhere. If you want to have an impact, I have been told time and again, you need a style that makes you visible. You have to be somewhat strident, intimidating, superaggressive."

However, Macklin said Blacks do value an androgynous style, preferring to do things through relationships rather than through bureaucratic structures. This tends to pull black people together into a "brotherhood network, even when we don't know each other." This basic difference in style also creates distrust. Macklin noted that white women believe black men have access to the male club. Although black men probably do get invited to lunch or for a drink after work by white males more often than women do, they lack access to the white male organizational network. Black men and white men tend to interact as individuals, not sharing networks. "These individual relationships do not bring black men much power," Macklin stated.

On Being a Woman and a Manager

The experiences of women managers coincide with those of Macklin as a black manager. The primary issues for women are gaining support for their minority position and respect for their organizational style and their competence as managers. Ellen Howe, one of the first woman warehouse managers at a large manufacturing company, described some of the differences between male and female organizational styles:

Department managers' meetings are so competitive. After a
while they become like a chess game. I can see the moves in
advance. My boss says something. Then someone comes back
with a zinger, starting the warfare. I don't deal that way, and I
continue to be amazed at how irrational men really are at work.
They can be so preoccupied about turf issues, and sometimes
they make speeches at each other in meetings and act as if they
are communicating. Whom do they think they are impressing,
anyway?

Some of the women I know deal differently; they seem less
concerned about winning. The result is that they are seen as less
powerful. The way we speak is different too. We have to repeat
what we say any number of times in order to be heard.

Howe also spoke of the recurring fight to win respect for her
competence as a manager:

I had to deal with male truck drivers from outside the plant on
shipping problems. They would ask me who was in charge,
who had the authority to make the decision. I would tell them
that I was the warehouse manager. They would say flatly, "I
don't believe you." It was too great a cultural shock for them.

Often, it seems, men expect women *not* to be competent. One
management consultant described her worst experience in working
with a man as follows: "I felt overpowered, put down, ignored,
treated as if I had nothing to offer. I had to prove I was competent,
and yet each time I did, it seemed like an isolated incident.
Gradually, I just began to withdraw rather than pushing myself out
into the fray." Another said, "My boss was highly threatened by my
clinical expertise and looked for ways to discredit me. Constant
conflict arose over office procedures, telephone calls—all kinds of
picayune things." While these events occur with male managers as
well, there is an additional problem if it's a male-female exchange.
The woman worries about whether conflict is arising because she's a

woman or because she's incompetent— either lacking the necessary skills or lacking political savvy about the organization.

The double load that black women carry was described by Elsie Cross, a black senior organization consultant in Philadelphia. She had to contend with being tested for competence as well as with being labeled militant or pushy:

> My experience with whites (both men and women) has often been quite abysmal. Before I entered management, I never knew how bad such experiences could be, and at first I blamed myself for not being smart enough or clear enough, or for being out of step. I have also had some truly wonderful experiences with whites through training/consulting relationships, usually when I have been in charge—as dean, as the primary link with a client, or as a teacher or trainer of professionals. Some of my most satisfying experiences have been in working with colleagues on issues relating to race and sex. We came together as peers to do training and consulting in these areas, and there was true collaboration. Working together in such relationships has been a freeing rather than a restricting experience.

Cross held out the hope for relationships in which colleagues showed respect for each other's competence as managers as well as showing concern and support for each other as people.

> I know several white women who, having worked on their sexism, have come to a profound understanding of racism. When I am with women who have empathy for and experience with people of color, it is like being in a family—knowing that we won't agree, or always like each other, but that there is trust and belief in each other. I feel accepted as an intelligent, competent human being and know we can fight and love and collaborate without being destructive. These women are also wonderful at being supportive and nurturant to me and allow me to be caring, loving, and supportive of them.

Women managers say time and again that tears are the result
of extreme frustration and inability to express what they feel.
Many male managers are unable to handle women's anger,
directness, frustration, and different ways of dealing with problems. So tears are usually the last resort. Also, most male
managers I have asked have not seen many women cry on the
job—they have not seen a lot of women at work in management
positions—and are terrified at the thought. Their fear seems to
me to be rooted in sexuality, potency, and dependency. What
they are really unable to handle are their own feelings, which
they project onto the women.

Many men say in one way or another, when they can really
be open and honest, how very much afraid they are of having to
compete—really compete—with women, Blacks, and other
people of color. The way things are arranged, they will never
have to compete with them in any real sense. They do say, at
times, that they are sorry for their juniors, who will be
competing.

Effective Relationships

Despite the conflicts in styles and expectations, there are satisfying relationships between men and women, minorities and whites,
in organizations. Many of the women I surveyed reported numerous
positive experiences working with men. They generally recalled as
positive those experiences in which they were respected, treated as
equal co-workers, and shown some empathy for their position as
women in organizations. They liked working with men who would
join them in challenging assignments. A number mentioned that the
best working relationships included fun. Sarah Risher, a training
consultant, stated, "My best experience was with a man who not
only recognized and accepted my capabilities but also encouraged
me—and even prodded me to do more."

Carol Gibson said her best interaction with a man at work

BARRIERS TO INTERACTION IN ORGANIZATIONS

involved the manager she replaced in an assignment. "Originally, we were both threatened by each other—he because a young woman was taking his position and me because he had so much knowledge of the job." However, the relationship developed into a "very open and warm one. We are direct and free in our feedback and thoughts."

Susan Schwab, an organization consultant for a large manufacturing corporation, said:

> The best interactions that I have with men at work, I believe, are the result of some subtle, perhaps unspoken, message that I receive that my input is valued and that I am looked upon as another competent person to design a program or a meeting, or to solve a problem. Then I can be fully me and allow my creativity to flow and blend with the man's. Synergy develops, and the results are always exciting and fun!

> When I am working with a man who seems to be testing me (and I work with a lot of professional interviewers), I feel myself become tense, and that blocks the flow of my creativity and energy in getting the work done. Women have to work so damn hard sometimes to get things done and to prove themselves.

> Last week at the staff meeting I felt accepted by the men more fully than I have in almost two and a half years of being the only woman (or one of the few women) attending. During the two days of meetings, I do not recall one man apologizing to me in some way for swearing! Now, to me that is progress.

It is obvious how much vitality and enthusiasm Susan brought to relationships. She also brought a sense of colleagueship, which surprised some men. As an illustration, Susan related the following experience:

> I would like to share one of my favorite stories about something that happened to me shortly after joining the company. We were finishing up late, and a male colleague and I were the last

ones to leave the meeting. I asked him if he had time for a drink before he went home. He looked down at his papers, shuffled them about a bit, and then said, "Gee, Susan, no. I have to go home and have a drink with my kids." I was halfway down the hall when I realized his kids were three and five and giggled to myself and also felt somewhat sad.

This same man brought up the incident at a lunch meeting (with four men at the table) several weeks later and told of talking it over with his wife when he got home. He said he never thought he would have been embarrassed by a woman asking him out for a drink, but when it actually happened, he was shook. He is a good colleague, has told this story about himself many times, and certainly has learned from the experience. During my first year with the company, he and his wife were the only ones to include me as a single woman at a party at their home.

Men also find that working with the other sex can be both difficult and delightful. Here are some examples of difficult experiences provided by the male management consultants I surveyed:

"Working with a female trainer who polarized staff around every issue, making each into a sexist issue."

"Being told by a woman colleague I respected and loved that my expression of love was inherently oppressive because it implied submission to me by her. Baloney!"

"Dealing with a woman who failed to do her job as secretary. When I attempted to relieve her, she claimed it was because she had refused my sexual advances. Everyone around knew that it was absurd, but it was annoying."

Men tend to like the same things about working with women that women do about working with men. One man reported that his best experiences included "good dialogue, equal confronting of each other, shared responsibility, good feedback both ways, fun, and high-quality work." Another reported a positive experience as "straightforward task accomplishment."

One man reported that his best work relationship was with a woman manager who exhibited androgynous behavior. He said she was "not only very task-competent but had a great sense for what I was feeling, often before I did, and helped me get in touch with that. Also, through listening and wise interpretation, she was able to help me sort out some interpersonal problems with other co-workers."

Finally, there is the reward for the woman manager who has passed the test. As Gibson said:

> After five years of working in this plant—that's longer than 80 percent of the male managers—I can share some "war stories" and have a list of experiences to pull from. Each of these abilities makes me more credible with the men, since sharing experiences and stories is much of the way of "getting in."

> I don't mean to sound egotistical by saying this; it's just that these experiences and my feelings surprise me. I never thought I would be able to say at some point that I had gotten beyond some of the pain and struggle that I felt would never cease. I know everything will not always be rosy, but experiencing this feeling now is grand—even if it's only for a limited time!

The comments by these managers—male and female—illustrate well the value of androgynous behavior in the workplace. For women, this often means being more assertive with both men and women; holding on to their expressive behavior; sharing discomforts and dealing with conflict; and asking for feedback.

For men, strengthening interactions in the organization means opening up; being more candid when the politics of the situation permit; and sharing their discomfort over the new situations into which they are being thrust. As one 50-year-old white male consultant said, "I am in more and more dissonance-producing situations with women and minorities and it doesn't always feel comfortable, but it sure does feel real!"

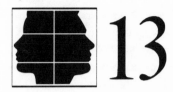

13

Sexuality in Organizations

Sexuality poses a special problem in the development of androgynous behavior. When men and women work together, the issue of sexual attraction is always present. It may be ignored, but it won't go away. Members of both sexes usually appraise each other sexually. They may or may not be attracted to each other, but the sexual issue is always there.

We write each other either on or off at some level in each male-female transaction. Having lunch or a drink together becomes a question of rejection versus acceptance between women and men rather than an act of colleagueship. When a female colleague refuses a dinner invitation by replying, "I'm too tired and need to prepare for tomorrow's meeting," this has a quality of rejection that would probably not exist if a man said he was too tired or busy to have dinner with another man.

Among the managers and consultants I surveyed, sexual issues seemed to concern men much more than women. Men often mentioned sexual complications with women as the "worst thing that could happen in a work situation with the other sex." Women rarely mentioned sexual issues. One hypothesis for this is that being the object of women's sexual advances is a new experience for a man. Women for years have been saying no to sexual overtures. Not only have men not had advances made as often, but saying no is inconsistent with their role expectations for performance. Sexually, men's worst fears in their relationships with women colleagues include displaying emotions and having sexual overtones develop; becoming emotionally involved in work relationships, which could destroy marriages; and getting caught having physical contact or making love.

One man said, "We could get involved in a personal, physical relationship due to lack of control on both our parts." Another said, "A woman who wanted to could do me considerable harm by circulating rumors accusing me of making advances." Interestingly, none of the men expressed concern that a physical relationship would actually hamper the work of the organization. In contrast, the U.S. Congress held hearings on the pervasiveness of sexual problems in federal agencies. Subsequently, the Office of Personnel Management (formerly the U.S. Civil Service Commission) issued instructions that, as part of management policy, the federal government as an employer must provide a workplace free of sexual harassment.

The issue from the male perspective was stated clearly by William J. Crockett, a consultant previously at the Saga Corporation:

> Being androgynous in my view is quite a different issue in relationships between a man and another man than in those between a man and a woman and may be easier to accomplish. Before most of us men can accept a woman associate as a fellow human being with whom we can share our feelings of care and concern, we first must work through our own male needs around the sex issue—that is, "Is she a potential conquest?" My view is that it is much more of an issue than most men admit, and therefore it is much more difficult for men to show their

androgynous nature to women associates than to men associates. Of course, this too can be worked out one way or another within a group over time, so that finally a man can relate to a woman on a personal level and not actually be making a sex-oriented overture or be afraid she or his associates will suspect him of it.

The women managers I interviewed were troubled much less by sexual issues than by the need to be taken seriously as professionals. They wanted to have their competence recognized and to be given the room to make full use of their talents. They described their best interactions with men as those that were professional, working partnerships with no sexual overtones. And they firmly believed that such partnerships were possible.

Thus the concerns of men and women in organizations today are often far apart. While women are worrying over whether they are being viewed as competent, men are often fretting about how to deal with sexual attraction or lack of it.

But the problem is more complicated. When I was working with the top women managers in one manufacturing corporation, they said, "You know, sex is just never an issue around here. None of the men ever talk about attraction or anything. What is going on?" These women were extremely attractive, forceful, and articulate. When I talked to the men, on the other hand, they said that the women were just too much to fight. It was not relaxing to have dinner with them on the road or to converse with them informally about the organization. Nor were the men willing to tell the women how their style turned them off. The lack of attraction cut these women out of a crucial information network that would have been valuable in their work. Instead, both the men and the women withdrew from professional and personal contact. Apparently, both sides felt that to mention sex would be to encourage or legitimize it rather than to objectify and diffuse it. More expressive communication—direct man-woman conversations about relaxing and being less uptight—might have defused sex as an issue and helped both sides make contact.

Traveling Together

Traveling together has been an approach-avoidance experience for men and women managers. Joint travel would seem to add interest to work, but it raises the issues of sexual attraction even more sharply, since there is ample opportunity to let go with fewer of the office norms in effect. Traveling highlights traditional views of the male-female relationship, so here more than elsewhere new values and attitudes are necessary to facilitate man-woman communication.

On one consulting trip, I arrived at the manufacturing plant early in the morning to be told that the plant manager had to see me right away. The emergency was that he was going to travel across country with a very attractive woman manager. He wanted to talk to me about how to tell his wife. After an hour and a half discussion, he decided he would not tell her. He traveled with the woman manager and made sexual advances. She refused him and protected him, never mentioning the incident to anyone but me, the external consultant. The poignant part was that the plant manager, who had married early in life, apparently had had very little experience with women. He was acting out of old norms that probably dated back 35 years, to his adolescence. He had not had ample opportunities to be attracted to women, tell them about it, have them tell him how they felt in return, and then discuss with them what they wanted to do about their feelings.

On the whole, the women managers I interviewed displayed a professional attitude toward working and traveling with male colleagues. They expressed concern about building new, mature work relationships with men. Their comments included:

> "Both of us, for whatever reason, have decided that sexual involvement is not a possibility."

> "We are very professional with each other."

> "Each person is secure about his or her own worth and strengths and is able to acknowledge the strengths of others and how these are

complementary; both people feel free to let their hair down with each other—to easily check out any concerns about sleeping arrangements, meals, and so on."

"I usually make my own arrangements for after-work hours—sometimes with peers, sometimes not. I'm careful not to establish patterns."

"When I travel with men, we go to meetings, then to dinner, perhaps dancing or drinking, and we talk rather personally. Often, there is also a quiet give-and-take and professional sharing."

"Each trip, I wait for the moment when the men try to slip away without me because they feel more comfortable with each other. At first, I used to let them go and felt bad about myself. I would order room service or get a hamburger by myself. I felt very lonely and angry, and I never knew what was going on as well as they did, so I started forcing myself to hang out with them. It's still rough and new, and I know they'd rather I didn't go along, but what are my choices? So I go."

"To me, the ideal relationship involves sharing the traveling workload and challenging and supporting each other. Disagreeing and fighting are OK, as well as expressions of tenderness and caring."

For most of these women, being treated as an equal is the most important aspect of the male-female work relationship. As one woman told me:

The man I worked closest with on most projects was a total co-equal. We traveled together often, allowed each other to utilize our individual talents with clients, and gave freely of praise and criticism. At the end of a day in another town, we could relax together—even occasionally order room service and watch television in one or another's room—with absolutely no sexual involvement. Neither of us was interested in spoiling a perfect working relationship. Sure, men have made passes at me in the work setting, but never those with whom I've first established a solid, mutually beneficial, and professional give-and-take.

Men too commented that they were striving to build new relationships with women at work—relationships that were often different from their relationships with women in their private lives. One manager said of a woman he often does business with: "We often meet together in other cities. We stick to our work usually, but share feelings very openly about work and some about more personal things. There is much respect and liking, although we carefully avoid anything explicitly sexual. Our relationship is a real joy."

Another man described a successful relationship with a woman colleague in a similar manner: "We are quite fond of each other but have no desire to be lovers. We can both use the other for comfort and counsel and respect one another's competence. We laugh a lot together."

Said another: "I do a lot of traveling with women. It's never been a problem. The women I travel with all want to be treated as equals, and I think I treat them as such."

Another manager who travels a lot expressed a different attitude: "I like to relax over dinner. There are only a couple of women in our place who travel with us. They're too serious. They like to talk about the company. I feel guilty, but some of us try to duck out before they ask us about our plans."

It is clear from these comments that the range of openness in relationships between male and female colleagues is vast. But in some cases a lot of adjustment is needed to get the relationship on a smooth footing where the man and woman can have fun together and relax.

Behind some of these complications are fears of spouses' perceptions. These may never get dealt with, particularly if the social patterns are such that at parties the wives cluster in one corner and the men in another, with the women who work in the organization going back and forth or talking only with the men. This process tends to inhibit open communication. Sexual stereotyping is more likely to flourish than to die, and the result may be a lot of fear and anxiety. In one plant the pressure of the sexual issue was such that the wives of some of the men did not want them to play in a tennis tournament against an attractive woman manager.

Working It Out

The management consultants I surveyed described situations in which they had worked out sexual issues satisfactorily. Generally, they dealt with these issues head on, with the full range of choices possible. Frequently, the consultant chose not to confuse a professional relationship with a personal relationship, although the attraction was quite strong. Both the men and the women indicated that when traveling together as well as working together in the office, they liked to share work and leisure in a spirit of mutual support. They were willing to discuss those issues with each other as well as with each other's spouse. It was not uncommon for consultants to go out of their way to meet each other's family. They wanted to know the spouse and the children, and they wanted the family to know them, in order to reduce some of the anxiety about traveling and spending so much time together.

It seems that men and women get along best at work and on business trips when sexual attraction is dealt with explicitly and then put aside as an issue. The best thing to do with the issue is to talk about it. If it stays hidden, it can cause much more damage than if it is confronted openly. Spouses can and should be involved in general discussions about these pressures. When everyone involved meets face to face, people can see each other as human beings, rather than as impersonal and threatening sex or success objects.

Members of both sexes want to be treated as competent and compassionate human beings. They need the support of others and want to have fun in their work relationships. Male-female relationships at work offer such a rich blend of androgynous behavior—of competence, warmth, support, and fun—that the negotiations and awkwardness necessary to make such relationships happen seem more than worthwhile.

14

Androgyny Beyond the Office

The concept of androgyny promises to have a substantial impact on people's lives at home as well as at work. As men develop new styles and less competitive friendships with other men, they will be liberated from their complete dependency on women to meet their emotional needs. And as women gain professional success and enjoy more fulfilling relationships with other women, they will be freed from their dependency on men to fulfill their needs for approval and ratification. Androgyny calls for an integration of roles and for adding new behaviors to men's masculinity and women's femininity. Many of these changes are already taking place. Men are learning to fry eggs, prepare baby bottles, and express vulnerability. Women are learning to change tires, write requests for proposals, and be more visible and assertive.

These changes are liberating for both sexes. As men learn androgynous behavior at work and at home, they begin to value themselves beyond their breadwinner capacity. They learn to appreciate themselves as whole people, making valuable contributions in both action and feeling. This can lead to an enhanced self-concept for men and to great fulfillment in all aspects of their lives.

Women, too, are strengthening their self-concept as they expand beyond the ties of home and hearth or receive greater respect for their contribution to the home environment. As men begin to share in household tasks, they learn that performing these tasks deserves recognition, and they often express greater admiration for their wives. Many men also report that they feel a greater sense of independence when they can cook for themselves or do their laundry. It is not unusual to hear a male manager in the course of a conversation with his wife report that he did his laundry. At the same time, women are gaining a great deal of satisfaction and self-esteem as they take on home responsibilities once reserved for men—such as handling the insurance, investing their income, and doing the taxes.

As recently as 1970, there was no question of who took care of the home: the woman did, regardless of whether she worked. Now, because of the increasing numbers of women moving into the workforce as well as a new attitude toward who does what in the home, men are becoming more active around the house. Marjorie Hansen Shaevitz and Morton Shaevitz, couples therapists and consultants in San Diego, point out that just as women have feelings of discomfort in certain parts of the workplace, men—although they grew up in a home—are often uncomfortable doing what heretofore has been called women's work. Their comfort may be dependent upon what their fathers did or what other men in their neighborhood now do, or what people at work say they do at home.

In *Making It Together* the Shaevitzes recommend three criteria for the allocation of work at home: availability, skill, and enjoyment. These criteria are very different from the ones that traditionally shaped the division of labor in the home. The Shaevitzes suggest that housework be divided into the following areas: household management; house maintenance; child-related activities; meals and cooking; yard work; automobiles; finances; health-related activities;

family and social relationships and events; vacation-related activities; religious activities; family pets; and emergencies.[1]

In his book *Passive Men, Wild Women*, Pierre Mornell, M.D., makes a pitch for men to be more active, involved, and responsible at home as well as to be better understood for their passivity, which often results from the stress they have undergone during the day in their professional lives. At the same time, women need to be understood for their "wildness," which stems from a long period of feeling unheard and unfulfilled. In his book, Mornell paints the picture of the man who is active, articulate, and energetic in his work, but who returns home at night inactive, inarticulate, and lethargic. He wolfs down his dinner, pays token attention to his family, and withdraws to the television set. Meanwhile, his wife, regardless of whether she has a career, wants "something more" in her intimate relationship. She wants to make contact, share experiences, feel more in touch with herself, feel confirmed as a person. Eventually, many wives become angry and depressed in the face of their husbands' withdrawal.[2]

Here again, we see the importance of androgynous behavior in the home as well as in the office. I have frequently noted the cool male/hysterical female syndrome among couples. It is as if the more she escalates in order to be heard, the more he withdraws, and that makes her "wild" and him "passive" in Mornell's description.

The feminist movement, dual-career families, and rising divorce rates have pulled the rug out from under old-style dependency relationships. Men and women are seeking their own satisfaction as individuals. They are no longer willing or able to carry the burden of each other's dependency. This means that men and women must develop within themselves and through their support systems the ability to fulfill their own needs. Men can begin learning to express emotions, with or without the help of a supportive female. They can redefine male friendships beyond the usual buddy or teammate concept, learning to value sensitivity and emotional support from male friends. Likewise, women can establish their own sense of achievement and their own women's networks without relying on

Did I Sound OK?

Natasha Josefowitz

Fifty people at the meeting——
I want to say something,
But is it relevant
And is it pertinent
And is this the time
Or should I wait?
Perhaps it's dumb
Or has been said.
I wish it were not so important
for me to sound clever
and original
whenever I talk
wanting every time
to make an important contribution
to the goings-on.
I hate wanting others
to respect me.
I hate caring so much
that I should be liked.
Why should it matter?
But it does.
Damn it, it *does!*
So with pounding heart
I say it——

Was it OK?
Tell me—how did I sound?

the achievements of the men who are close to them. Once men and women learn how to satisfy their own needs, they can develop their relationships as two whole and fulfilled people who want to share their lives, rather than as dependent "halves" looking to each other to become complete.

It seems likely that relationships between men and women, in or out of the office, will become more natural as people acquire greater capacities for androgynous behavior. This will remove the pressure of the game and the trauma of the unknown. It will allow men and women to relate according to their circumstances rather than their sex-role perceptions. Relationships can be more direct, communicative, and fulfilling if they are based on connections between healthy rather than needy men and women.

It is essential that new mechanisms be designed swiftly to assist people through the transitions and upheaval in their roles. The marketplace has for too long left to the individual employee the burden of reconciling discrepancies between personal needs and work needs. Public policies are critically needed to reduce the conflict: flexible and reduced working hours, job sharing, two years' time to plan for a job relocation, assistance from the organization in, finding jobs for spouses in a new locale, new career paths, management development programs for women over 35, and relief from nightshift work for single heads of households.

In sharp contrast to the United States, Sweden has well-established public policies which recognize that adults will both work and raise families, and that there is sufficient time in one lifetime to do both. Swedish policies include a parenthood insurance fund, much like workers' compensation, that gives the father or the mother a parenthood leave of absence with pay during the first six months after a child is born. In addition, a family may take 12 to 18 days off per years with pay to take care of sick children. In the next eight years of the child's life, parents may work six-hour days so they have more time at home.[3] Another Swedish public policy that supports the family is the law against parents hitting children.

In America such policies, though badly needed, are barely in their infancy. As Herman Gadon, professor of organizational behavior at San Diego State University, notes:

> Alternative work schedules provide men and women with opportunities to be treated like a whole person, to integrate their personal lives with the demands of work. Six years of study have shown that alternative work schedules are more than a modest fringe benefit offered at relatively low cost. They represent significant changes in the structure of work, leading to higher productivity as well as to greater satisfaction on the job. Alternative work schedules include flextime, compressed workweeks, job sharing, and permanent part-time work.
>
> *Flextime* is already a substantial factor in the computer industry, e.g. Hewlett Packard, Control Data, Digital Equipment; insurance firms, e.g. John Hancock, Metropolitan Life; and government agencies, e.g. Social Security, Geological Survey; and it is spreading steadily throughout the private and public sectors. *Permanent part-time work* has been used for some time in many service industries, e.g. retailing and small-freight handling; and is being tried in insurance, banking, and government organizations. *Job sharing* is still in its infancy, and compressed workweeks are now showing limited growth. Organizations are still experimenting with new arrangements. Because flexibility offers so many advantages to individuals and organizations, alternative work schedules seem certain to become commonplace before the year 2000.[4]

In addition to the lack of supportive public or business policy for workers, support systems for spouses and couples are rare in our country. Several corporations have minimal programs for spouses —possibly six sessions to explain health benefits, mobility policies, and the impact of affirmative action on the company. Very few training programs, except at the executive level, take the spouse into account.

One exemplary program was developed by Barrie Grieff, psychiatrist at the Harvard Business School.[5] Grieff gives a course entitled "The Executive Family Seminar," designed to deal with business students' complaints that the rigors of work cut into their marriages. Grieff often heard of the angry, jealous spouse who was frustrated by having to compromise his or her needs for the sake of "their career." The seminar focuses on:

1. Examining relationships among the individual, the family, and the organization.
2. Helping couples recognize that they do not have to capitulate to external events but can be active in designing their individual, marital, and corporate lives.
3. Studying the normal, dynamic development of talented, aggressive, and perceptive couples engaged in the business world (those accepting a high degree of risk and mobility).
4. Exploring the trade-offs as couples become more intimately involved in their personal and professional lives.
5. Analyzing the myths of marriage, and examining the critical points in the life cycle.
6. Giving couples the opportunity to interact with other couples in order to share experiences.

Among the topics discussed are the role of women in business; business travel and job relocation; dealing with success; the impact of job loss on a family; the dual-career couple; the decision to have or not have children; the executive living abroad; divorce; extramarital affairs; and the psychological manifestations of stress. Implicit in Grieff's course is the importance of an equal partnership in which both husband and wife are highly valued and focus on the process as well as the activities of their relationship.

The support mechanisms necessary to maintain relationships in our increasingly complex culture are vast. Organizations and public policy have a long way to go to provide the much needed assistance to people facing conflicts between work and home—conflicts that they should not have to deal with by themselves.

NOTES

1. Marjorie Hansen Shaevitz and Morton H. Shaevitz, *Making It Together* (Boston: Houghton-Mifflin, 1980).
2. Pierre Mornell, M.D., *Passive Men, Wild Women* (New York: Simon & Schuster, 1979).
3. "Fact Sheet on Sweden," January 1979. Published by the Swedish Institute and available through the Swedish Information Service, 825 Third Avenue, New York, N.Y. 10022.
4. Allan R. Cohen and Herman Gadon, *Alternative Work Schedules: Integrating Individual and Organizational Needs* (Reading, Mass.: Addison-Wesley, 1978).
5. Barrie Grieff, "The Executive Family Seminar: A course for Graduate Married Business Students," *Journal of the American College Health Association*, Vol. 24, No. 4 (April 1976). Also found in Barrie Sanford Grieff and Preston K. Munter, *Trade-offs: Executive, Family, and Organization Life* (New York: Simon & Schuster, 1979).

Toward an Androgynous Organization

Behavioral science researchers and management theorists have put forth various criteria for organizational effectiveness and health. According to Peter Drucker, healthy organizations are managed by "results and self-control." An executive in Drucker's organization uses time carefully, is oriented toward results rather than work, develops subordinates, establishes priorities, and makes decisions. Rensis Likert defined System IV, a participative model, as the most productive. Robert Blake and Jane Mouton claimed the "9,9" leadership style—equal concern for task and people—was superior to others. Chris Argyris defined effective organizations as open and process-oriented as opposed to competitive and closed. David McClelland implied that the healthy organizational climate includes achievement, power, and affiliation rewards.

Several of these models have tended to be normative and prescriptive, but they also are models of androgynous organizations. In making organizational changes, the management consultant's first principle is "Start where the client is," particularly with the client's dissatisfaction about the current organization. The move toward androgynous organizations involves changing a small chunk at a time, where there is a champion for the change. To attempt to convert suddenly and completely to androgyny would be a contradiction in itself. When organizations have tried to change everything at once, they have rarely been successful. For example, with MBO or ZBB, employees have choked trying to digest the model like a snake swallowing an elephant, or else they have resisted the whole process. The goal is to spell out components and choose from the array. Androgyny is intended to broaden our options for behavior, not to be a prescriptive or normative model.

The issue, as stated by Alice Mack, a consultant in Denver, is the urgent necessity of integrating masculine and feminine values, traits, and behaviors into ourselves and then slowly into organizational structures and processes. The "healthy" person, as described by psychologists, is a mixture of masculine and feminine characteristics. Similarly, the healthy organization, as researched and substantiated by management and behavioral scientists over the last 30 years, is a male-female balance between task and people.

As emphasized throughout this book, organizations need their own model of an effective manager as well as criteria for organizational effectiveness. The androgynous manager combines rational problem-solving competencies and interpersonal competencies, including both compliance-producing and alliance-producing skills. The androgynous manager also has the skill to build an organizational environment that balances concern for achievement and power with concern for affiliation needs.

There is, of course, the question of which comes first: managers who are ready to utilize a mix of masculine and feminine skills or organizations that value and foster the development of such skills. At a time when human resources development is vital to the life of organizations, we cannot wait to see who makes the first move. Organizations need to promote a full range of skills among all managers, and, at the same time, managers need to demonstrate their interest in and readiness to expand their behaviors.

Defining Androgynous Behavior

The pervasiveness of white male management styles was reflected in the answers that many men and women gave to the question of what skills and behaviors they felt they would need to become more androgynous. Women as well as men often said that they needed to become more expressive, more skilled at listening, and less threatened by failure. When asked what additional qualities they would like to acquire in order to increase their managerial effectiveness, women respondents often listed such male characteristics as increased assertiveness, problem-solving skills, and analytical abilities. Of course, some male respondents went the other way: they wanted to develop collaborative styles and human relations skills.

One management consultant said that to become more androgynous he would need to become more expressive and to exhibit "more open caring for others." When asked what qualities he wanted to acquire to increase his managerial effectiveness, he listed problem solving, "particularly diagnostic skills," first. Another man said he would like to use his intuition more effectively as a source of direction for solutions to messy problems.

Carol Gibson, the department head, listed several characteristics she felt would make her a more effective manager. The list included empathy, patience, firmness, gentleness, compromise, honesty, confrontation, assertiveness, respect for others, and sensitivity to feelings—a combination of masculine and feminine behaviors.

Lee Porach, a woman management consultant, said, "In an androgynous system, I would be more open in expressing feelings and emotions. I would be more willing to give males constructive feedback. I would be more trusting of men."

Many women stressed acting more assertively in their dealings with bosses, colleagues, and subordinates. One said she would like to be able to "confront and support simultaneously and competently." Another said she would like to be "more assertive, more direct, less wary of the label 'pushy broad.'"

To the consultants I surveyed, I posed the question, "What would need to be done in the marketplace to encourage more androgynous behavior?" One woman consultant answered, "I see a need for it to be legitimate for women to be as assertive and aggressive as men. Women in general still do the caretaking, psyching out men to get what they want. It works, but it infuriates me." Another woman responded, "I'd need to stop being punished for assertive, leaderlike behavior and start being rewarded for it more than I am now. I don't need permission; I just need not to be punished—and, by the way, rewards would be nice too."

Other conditions women thought were necessary to feel comfortable expressing androgynous behaviors included:

"A high value placed on intuition."

"A climate in which I wouldn't have to worry about being perceived as a woman first, a manager second."

"Just as many women in management positions as men."

"An organizational value placed on being individualistic."

The male consultants surveyed spoke of placing a higher value on human qualities as the key to encouraging androgynous behavior. For example, in order to become more androgynous at work, Stan Hinckley, an organization consultant in Cincinnati, said he would need "recognition that human problems are as important as task problems and that a good manager is expected to handle both types well."

Others spoke of current managerial attitudes that inhibit androgynous behavior:

"Management is critical of swings of emotions."

"A gut feel is not OK. In addition to laying out all the facts, a presentation must be devoid of feeling."

"A manager needs to be strong and nurturing to be effective with

employees. Yet this is not seen as having much to do with results. All these attitudes are quite stifling."

"I would like to work in a place where I could feel more comfortable being free with feelings generally—more spontaneous, more happy, more sad, more excited."

The struggle to be androgynous, especially to evidence the feminine side of androgyny in the managerial marketplace, can take its toll. Women particularly question themselves. After making it, one woman wondered:

Have I copped out or have I matured as a professional business-woman? On my last performance appraisal, they asked me why I no longer was the fighter, taking charge, raising the issues. I'm taking better care of myself—the company doesn't own me anymore.

Part of the change is that I now feel more mature. But it's still a real dilemma to me. I feel like maybe I'm buying into the male norms and style of operating, and that feels uncomfortable to me. I still struggle to find the balance between being perceived by the "system" as effective and successful and maintaining my own style and my femininity.

The Organization's Role

An organization that wishes to promote androgynous management is confronted with three major tasks:

1. Developing a *climate* that creates the opportunity for value shifts, behavior change, and skills development.
2. Developing *strategies* that require and encourage androgynous management competencies.
3. Developing *reward systems* that reinforce these competencies.

The proper climate makes it possible for people to grow and change;

the development of new strategies and reward systems motivates employees and managers to implement change.

Climate Setting

The organizational climate that promotes androgynous management is no different from one that typically generates opportunities for human resources development and organizational vitality. The characteristics of such a climate are (1) learning from new ideas and growth; (2) a concern for the interaction between task and people; (3) a continual search for improvement; and (4) a concern for the fit between organizational and individual goals, values, rewards, and developmental needs. These elements are congruent with those of a vital business:

- Provision of meaningful opportunities and incentive for work (achievement motivation).
- Sets of clearly communicated demands and exciting goals with as little red tape as possible (achievement motivation).
- Encouragement of relationships and networks that are constructive and stimulating (affiliation motivation).
- Support of attitudes of independence and self-reliance (personal power motivation).
- Established lines of authority and influence without unjust control (position power motivation).

Because human resources management can play such a vital role in androgynous management, the organizational climate needs to reflect a high concern for the individual, the work team, the organization, and the relationship with the external environment. Managers at all levels can be involved in improving the quality of organizational life, but they need to know that such an effort is important to the organization as a whole.

Strategies for Encouraging Androgynous Behaviors

A wide variety of human resources management strategies are available for organizations to encourage androgynous behaviors.

These strategies may involve establishing new organizational policies and practices, restructuring jobs to provide increased teamwork, improving working conditions, giving employees an opportunity to participate in setting goals and scheduling work, and increasing employee effectiveness through quality circles or other mechanisms designed to enhance satisfaction of personal needs.

Human resources practices in organizations often relate to how those resources are utilized—for example, programs of flexible working hours, training and development, participatory decision making, and job rotation. Other strategies aimed at human resources management focus on economic incentives—such as linking pay more clearly to performance rather than to longevity or to an institutionalized bonus system, effective policies on travel and mobility, and good fringe benefits regarding maternity or paternity leave.

Individual need fulfillment is a rich and controversial area. The challenge for organizations is to establish programs that promote personal growth, advancement, learning, achievement, meaningful interaction with others, positive feedback, recognition for performance, and participation. Managers are unlikely to develop androgynous behaviors at work unless institutional changes reward such efforts. If the organization emphasizes a firefighting approach based on competition and independence, managers simply may not have the time or energy left to experiment with collaboration and interdependence. Some managers may feel that they cannot risk losing the rewards that are predictably reaped through successful competition. In the long run competition may lead to dysfunctional stress among co-workers or units and potentially to hostility, as well as to missed opportunities for collaboration.

Furthermore, managers are unlikely to use androgynous skills to nurture and develop their subordinates without the clear encouragement of organizational policies. Many training and development consultants would agree that, left to their own devices, managers generally have difficulty finding time to become heavily involved in developing subordinates. Employee development requires contributing to the long-range growth of the company, and that does not fit in with the short-range results by which many middle managers are evaluated.

Rewarding Androgynous Management Practices

Another way that organizations can encourage androgynous management is by appropriately rewarding such behavior. Such rewards should include both informal praise and formal performance appraisal. Policymakers at the very top can encourage other managers by recognizing their efforts with statements like "I appreciated the openness and candor you brought to the meeting; you seemed to encourage everyone to air his or her feelings honestly," and "The personal sensitivity you are contributing to the job seems to be helping your employees develop quickly."

Many incentive plans themselves emphasize collaboration. Forms of direct worker ownership—including profit sharing, allowing all

---

A People Place

William J. Crockett (with thanks to Ken Medena)

If this is not a place where tears are understood,
   Where do I go to cry?
If this is not a place where my spirits can take wing,
   Where do I go to fly?
If this is not a place where my questions can be asked,
   Where do I go to seek?
If this is not a place where my feelings can be heard,
   Where do I go to speak?
If this is not a place where you'll accept me as I am,
   Where can I go to be?
If this is not a place where I can try to learn and grow,
   Where can I just be me?
If this is not a place where tears are understood,
   Where can I go to cry?

employees in a unit to share in the savings of their increased productivity, and labor-management committees—are being tried in more than 1,000 firms across the country, according to the National Center for Economic Alternatives in Washington, D.C.

Some work units in federal agencies are experimenting with using a percentage of pay as incentive to an entire work group rather than to individual employees in order to promote interdependence and offset the competitiveness that a merit system fosters. Another approach allows teams of employees to leave work early or take a day off when a certain amount of work is completed.

One large corporation that has been innovative in the field of career development has a coordinator of new managers. If an experienced manager is willing to take responsibility for "growing" a new manager, he or she contracts to do so for a six-month period. The new manager's salary is paid for out of the corporate budget. The contract may be renewed for up to two years, and the experienced manager is seen as providing a service to the organization. These approaches foster teamwork and its concomitant skills of collaboration and affiliation.

The criteria listed in performance review forms should include those that encourage feminine as well as masculine qualities. These might include such items as:

"Takes a personal interest in employees and their development."

"Is sensitive to employee needs and problems."

"Is able to assert position through well-reasoned arguments."

"Is able to collaborate with colleagues in other divisions."

"Takes initiative and is proactive."

"Actively assists the organization in meeting its affirmative action goals."

"Is effective in developing people from different ethnic backgrounds."

Another step that organizations can take to monitor their progress is to conduct periodic climate surveys about their own effectiveness. Here, too, criteria of effectiveness need to be reviewed for masculine and feminine dimensions. While the assignment of sex typing may at times be arbitrary, it is critical to make sure that feminine behaviors are not systematically ignored.

Building an androgynous organization requires that the manager move beyond developing androgynous behaviors to becoming an agent of change. In this case the manager becomes a visible role model as well as a systems designer for assessment practices, training programs, performance appraisal systems, and strategies for improving the organizational climate.

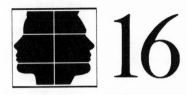

16

Developing Androgynous Managers

Androgyny is an integrating concept for the many different fields covered in this book, including human resources management; stress management; management competencies; new relationships between men and women, men and men, and women and women in organizations; and the interaction between family and work. The problems that exist in these areas are a long way from being solved. In some instances they are only just coming into consciousness.

The first step in the move toward androgyny is increasing awareness, and this book has been directed to that end. The book proposes a model of androgynous behavior. Achieving widespread acceptance of that model may take a long time—and it may take even longer to put supports in place to maintain the new androgynous behavior. But the effort, as we have seen throughout this book, is more than worthwhile.

All efforts to foster change involve many levels: an individual level, a peer group level, an organizational level, and a public policy level. One significant approach you can take as an individual—one that cuts across a number of levels—is to work on clarifying the management competencies valued in your organizational unit. Review the model in place for defining an effective manager. Evaluate the kinds of people who are promoted, and the information disseminated through training programs. Assess to what extent those competencies incorporate masculine and feminine behaviors, and raise questions if the feminine competencies are by and large ignored. As we have seen in earlier chapters, effective management in the 1980s requires a blend of compliance-producing and alliance-producing skills. It is critical to your organization that this blend be reflected in its assessment criteria, its training and development programs, and its performance evaluation system.

Strategies for Change

There are numerous strategies today for making personal changes. Below is a list compiled with the assistance of Donald Miller, previously of IBM:[1]

1. *Identifying*
   Identify the area in which you want to change.
2. *Sensing*
   Gather information.
   Set aside time for reflection.
   Become aware of a difference.
   Analyze what accepting new data may mean.
   Seek counsel to help you understand what is wrong.
   Be clear about those aspects of yourself that you won't change.
   Stay in touch with your values.
3. *Preparing*
   Give yourself a reason.
   Decide to change.
   Build a support group and meet with members regularly to
      share your perceptions of the need for change.
   Study your needs and work to increase your capabilities.

Deliberately make a change in some other aspect of your life to remind you of your goal. (For example, you might make a lifestyle change or a change in your dress or appearance.)

4. *Doing*

Let go.

Immerse yourself in the changed environment and find acceptance.

Stay in touch with your support system.

Establish subgoals and get feedback on your progress.

Modify your direction, if necessary, and implement further change.

As a first step in your efforts to move toward a more androgynous style, you might analyze the forces encouraging you to change as well as those restraining you. The force-field analysis shown in Figure 16-1 outlines some of the possible factors. The model is based on the work of social scientist Kurt Lewin, who postulates a process of unfreezing, changing, and refreezing as a way of breaking old adaptation patterns. According to Lewin, a person's current state is one of equilibrium in a field of driving and restraining forces—forces for or against a change in behavior. Lewin's notion implies the need to remove the restraining forces rather than add more driving forces in order to make a change.[2] Increasing the driving forces creates the risk that compensating restraining forces will develop.

Figure 16-1. Force-field analysis of androgynous behavior.

Driving Forces	Restraining Forces
"I'd have less stress."	"My spouse needs me to behave this way."
"I'd feel more comfortable being able to acknowledge my needs and vulnerabilities."	"I'm afraid of being ridiculed by other men (or women)."
"I'm tired of playing roles."	"My parents like me this way."
"Work would be more fun."	"I've worked hard to develop my style. I don't want to give it up."

Role Models and Support Systems

Another key step you can take toward becoming an androgynous manager is to cast about for role models for specific behaviors. There are few "new men" and "new women" to emulate, but some men are nurturant and some women are assertive.

Typically, men have an easier time identifying managerial role models than do women, since the scarcity of female managers—androgynous or otherwise—makes for fewer potential models. On the other hand, male role models are generally selected for their success in a typically male managerial mode—tough, independent, achievement-oriented, and so forth. It is more difficult to identify a successful male model who is also caring, expressive, and empathic.

One of the most significant steps in the move toward androgyny is building a support system for change. A support system is a resource pool drawn on selectively to support a person's effort at change and to leave the person stronger in the process.

Support systems are valuable sources of encouragement and assistance for any kind of personal change. Friends, family, and colleagues are good sounding boards for ideas and can be used for various types of support. For example, family and friends may be the best people with whom to vent crises of self-confidence, while colleagues at work may be best for giving you frank feedback on your performance. The key is to let somebody in. Don't try to go it alone when making personal changes. Sharing the fact that you are trying out a new personal style can lead to rewarding confirmation. For men, especially, learning to share feelings is part of the move toward androgyny.

Charles Seashore, a consultant in Washington, D.C., has conducted training programs on developing support systems. He emphasizes the importance of keeping a support system up to date and relevant to our goals. To do so, we must regularly assess the kinds of people who are available, let go of those who are not relevant or who in fact are sabotaging our efforts, and build in new people who can be of assistance. According to Seashore, support systems can be used in several different ways:

1. *To reestablish competence.* In times of high stress or major transitions, we may find ourselves functioning at a very low level of competence. This may be the result of anxiety, insufficient energy to cope with a crisis, physical or emotional difficulties, or an overload of demands put on us by other people. A good support system can help us cope and return to our previous level of functioning.

2. *To maintain high performance.* It is important to have access to resourceful people when we are doing well in order to maintain our high level of activity. It is often easier to profit from assistance when performance is high, yet many people neglect their support systems and find it more difficult to ask for help at such times.

3. *To gain new competencies.* A somewhat different function of support systems is to assist us in developing new skills. What we need here are people who can challenge us, serve as teachers and models, and provide emotional support when we feel awkward or inept in dealing with new situations.

4. *To achieve specific objectives.* Many objectives cannot be met without collaboration and contributions from people who have the skills and resources that we lack or do not wish to develop.

Seashore also proposes six key principles for establishing and maintaining support systems:

1. *Parsimony.* Keep the system as simple as possible to minimize the energy it takes to maintain it.

2. *Maintenance.* Keep relationships current and up to date so that, when people are needed, they are informed and appreciative of their relevance.

3. *Equity.* Establish relationships that are fair to both sides. Equity can be accomplished by reciprocal help, payment of money, joint sense of accomplishment, or whatever else makes sense. Guilt can easily build up when there is a feeling of indebtedness that cannot be repaid. It is important to be clear about each person's self-interest.

4. *External support base.* Keep the primary base of support outside the system in which your skills are being used. This will enable you to act autonomously and to engage in conflict when necessary. Leaning on people inside the system often leads to dependency. Paradoxically, when you have an external support group, people inside the system are more likely to be supportive. A good therapist can also be an important source of support and can be your champion in your effort to change. (It is important to emphasize that interviewing a number of therapists to find an effective one is critical. Androgynous therapists are probably as hard to come by as androgynous managers.)

5. *Backup .resources.* Maintain several sources for each kind of support you need to reduce your sense of vulnerability when someone is unavailable or unwilling to help in a given circumstance.

6. *Feedback.* Feedback is important to check on how members of the support group feel about giving or receiving assistance. The helping process often creates resistance or resentment. Unless people keep track of their feelings, the support relationship is likely to erode over time.

Figure 16-2, developed by Seashore, outlines several common personal problems and the relevant sources of support for dealing with them.

Support from the Other Sex

The most effective form of assistance in the move toward androgyny involves men and women working together to change. In addition, men need to work with other men, and women with other women, to share their feelings and express their needs. In mixed groups, men and women should discuss openly what they would like to learn from each other, genuinely listen to each other, test out new behaviors, and ask for feedback. Such an arrangement requires a great deal of trust, and the one who is first to suggest it may feel awkward. Often, a group meeting with an outside consultant can help start the process in a relatively risk-free manner.

In many cases, men who excel at directness, assertiveness, and task achievement can help women learn to value and acquire these skills. Similarly, women can help men understand and develop such skills as empathic listening, expression of feelings, and open communication. Much of this assistance can be informal and incidental, taking place as one person watches another closely, listens, and takes note of how certain behaviors work favorably in certain situations. However, more deliberate assistance is often more valuable. This includes men inviting women to meetings where they can learn from seeing how others operate, and women inviting themselves to such meetings. And it includes women expressing personal feelings and concern for others when men are present so that men can see the value of such expression.

Figure 16-2. Types of support systems.

Problem	Relevant Type of Support	Resolution
Confusion about future	Role models who demonstrate the opportunities and problems	Clarity
Social isolation	Networking People who share common interests	Social integration
Personal isolation	Close friends who are nurturant	Intimacy and caring; loss of alienation
Vulnerability	Helpers who can be depended on in a crisis	Expert assistance
Low self-esteem	Respectors of one's competence and skills	Higher esteem
Environmental isolation (resources unknown)	Referral agents Networking	Connections with resources
Stimulus isolation	Challengers to motivate development of new skills	Perception and energy

The change process starts internally, through some sense of dissonance between one's needs and desires and the realities of one's life. As the sense of dissatisfaction deepens, a person may choose to move beyond awareness to action. The effort to change requires support, reinforcement, and follow-up booster shots if it is to become more than a tentative exercise. The status quo always beckons with its comfortable, albeit sloppy familiarity. We need lots of props, reminders, and encouragement if we are to move through the discomfort of growth to the greater freedom of androgynous behavior.

NOTES

1. Donald B. Miller, *Personal Vitality* (Reading, Mass.: Addison-Wesley, 1977).
2. Kurt Lewin, *Field Theory in Social Science* (New York: Harper & Row, 1951).

Appendix A
The Androgyny Scale

Bem Sex-Role Inventory (BSRI)*

On the following page you will be shown a large number of personality characteristics and will be asked to use those characteristics in order to describe yourself. That is, you will be asked to indicate, on a scale of 1 to 7, how true of you these various characteristics are. Please do not leave any characteristic unmarked.

Example: Sly

Mark a 1 if it is *never or almost never true* that you are sly.
Mark a 2 if it is *usually not true* that you are sly.
Mark a 3 if it is *sometimes but infrequently true* that you are sly.
Mark a 4 if it is *occasionally true* that you are sly.
Mark a 5 if it is *often true* that you are sly.
Mark a 6 if it is *usually true* that you are sly.
Mark a 7 if it is *always or almost always true* that you are sly.

Thus, if you feel it is *sometimes but infrequently true* that you are "sly," *never or almost never true* that you are "malicious," *always or almost always true* that you are "irresponsible," and *often true* that you are "carefree," you would rate these characteristics as follows:

Sly	3	Irresponsible	7
Malicious	1	Carefree	5

*Reproduced by permission from *Beyond Sex Roles*, by Alice G. Sargent. Excerpt from "Psychological Androgyny," by Sandra Lipsitz Bem. Copyright © 1977, West Publishing Co. All rights reserved.

DESCRIBE YOURSELF

1	2	3	4	5	6	7
Never or almost never true	Usually not true	Sometimes but infrequently true	Occasionally true	Often true	Usually true	Always or almost always true

Self-reliant 5

Yielding 4

Helpful 6

Defends own beliefs 5

Cheerful 5

Moody 6

Independent 6

Shy 5

Conscientious 5

Athletic 7

Affectionate 7

Theatrical 5

Assertive

Flatterable

Happy 5

Strong personality

Loyal

Unpredictable

Forceful

Feminine

Reliable

Analytical 5

Sympathetic 6

Jealous 4

Has leadership abilities 6

Sensitive to needs of others 7

Truthful 5

Willing to take risks 6

Understanding 6

Secretive 6

Makes decisions easily

Compassionate

Sincere

Self-sufficient

Eager to soothe hurt feelings

Conceited

Dominant

Soft-spoken

Likable

Masculine

Warm

Solemn

Willing to take a stand

Tender

Friendly

Aggressive

Gullible

Inefficient

Acts as a leader

Childlike

Adaptable

Individualistic

Does not use harsh language

Unsystematic

Competitive

Loves children

Tactful

Ambitious

Gentle

Conventional

Scoring the Androgyny Scale

1. Score adjectives as follows:
   (a) The first adjective and every third one thereafter is masculine (for example, *masculine*—self-reliant). Mark these adjectives with an *M*.
   (b) The second adjective and every third one thereafter is feminine (*feminine*—yielding). Mark these adjectives with an *F*.
   (c) The third adjective and every third one thereafter is neutral (*neutral*—helpful). Mark these adjectives with an *N*.

To check yourself, see that the following words are marked:
   M   self-reliant
   N   reliable
   F   warm
   N   conventional

2. Calculate Masculinity and Femininity Scores by adding your numerical ratings for the 20 *M*'s to get the *M* total and your numerical ratings for the 20 *F*'s to get the *F* total. The number may be around 100. Ignore the *N*'s.

3. Divide: $\frac{M}{20}$ and $\frac{F}{20}$. Put each answer in decimal form.

4. Subtract *M* from *F*. If the Masculinity Score is larger, the result will be a negative number. If the Femininity Score is larger, the result will be a positive number.

5. Mark your Androgyny Score on the following continuum:

−3 −2 −1	−.5 −.9	−.5 0 +.5	+.5 +.9	+1 +2 +3
Masculine Type	Near Masculine Type	Androgynous Type	Near Feminine Type	Feminine Type

Discussion of the Score

The Masculinity and Femininity Scores indicate the extent to which a person endorses masculine and feminine personality characteristics as self-descriptive. As indicated above, the scores are simply the means of each subject's ratings of the masculine and feminine adjectives on the BSRI. Both these scores can range from 1 to 7. It should be noted that these two scores are logically independent. That is, the structure of the test does not constrain them in any way, and they are free to vary independently.

In contrast, the Androgyny Score (computed as Femininity minus Masculinity) reflects the relative amounts of masculinity and femininity that the person includes in his or her self-description, and, as such, it best characterizes the nature of the person's total sex role. Thus, if a person's Femininity Score is much higher than his or her Masculinity Score (that is, if a person describes himself as being much more feminine than masculine), then we think of that person as having a feminine sex role. Similarly, if a person's Masculinity Score is much higher than his or her Femininity Score, then we think of that person as having a masculine sex role. In contrast, if a person's Masculinity and Femininity Scores are approximately equal (that is, if there is really no difference in how masculine or feminine a person thinks he is), then we think of that person as having an androgynous sex role. A feminine sex role thus represents not only the endorsement of feminine attributes but the simultaneous rejection of masculine attributes. Similarly, a masculine sex role represents not only the endorsement of masculine attributes but the simultaneous rejection of feminine attributes. In contrast, an androgynous sex role represents the equal endorsement of both masculine and feminine attributes.

The specific masculine characteristics were selected because they were judged by a large sample of undergraduates to be more desirable in American society for a man than for a woman, and the specific feminine characteristics were selected because they were judged to be more desirable in American society for a woman than for a man.

Androgynous behavior is not the norm for our culture. Thirty-five percent of Sandra Bem's sample of Stanford University students were androgynous, 50 percent of that population were same-sex typed, and 15 percent were cross-sex typed. Those who were cross-sex typed were mostly women who had masculine behaviors. In my experience, professional women score much higher than nonprofessional women on the cross-sex typed scale. That is, they tend to be "near masculine" types. Very few professional men or male students have feminine behavior, and those who do experience a lot of conflict.

Bem set up two experimental situations to examine the implications of a high level of sex typing, as determined by the scores on her sex-role inventory. One experiment was designed to test "masculine" behavior (independence), and the other was designed to test "feminine" behavior (spontaneity, playfulness, and nurturance). In the first test, Bem invited subjects to participate in what they thought was an experiment on humor. The subjects were shown a series of cartoons, half of which were funny and half of which were very unfunny. Participants were requested to rate the cartoons after hearing, through a set of earphones, how others (their peers) had rated them. People with masculine or androgynous scores on the sex-role inventory were more likely to respond differently from their peers. People with feminine scores on the sex-role inventory capitulated, conforming to the others' ratings. When debriefed, they said, in effect, "You know, we didn't always go along with what we heard, but who are we to question?" The Bem study points out that there are costs to sex-typed behavior. Those who score high on feminine behavior may not feel free to disagree. They may conform and not behave independently in a situation where someone else, not necessarily even an authority figure, tells them something that they think is wrong.

In the second experiment, Bem told all the subjects that they were in a waiting room and that the experiment would take place outside the room. A baby and a kitten were in the room. Bem observed through a one-way mirror to see who touched, held, made eye contact with, or interacted in any other way with the baby or the kitten. In this situation, those with masculine behavior scores interacted very little with the baby or kitten. Whether they were unwilling to display the tender emotions they were experiencing or whether they were sufficiently inhibited that they did not experience such emotions is not known, according to Bem. In fact, the male response is closely related to the stress style of masculine types who perform tasks in good linear fashion, without being concerned with or attuned to feelings.

The androgynous people interacted more with the baby and kitten than did the masculine types. But those with feminine scores did not. They all saw the baby and kitten, but said they didn't know whether they could get up and go play with them because they were waiting to participate in the experiment. In this ambiguous situation, as in the first experiment, people with strong feminine behaviors were reluctant to take the initiative for fear of going against the authority in the situation, taking a risk, or simply doing what came naturally. Those with more feminine behavior appear hampered in their ability to deal with ambiguous situations, and that certainly is very costly behavior in the marketplace.

Appendix B
Sample Lists of Management Competencies

This appendix includes a listing of competencies from the following sources: (1) Overseas Private Investment Corporation (OPIC); (2) Pedler, Burgoyne, and Boydell; (3) U.S. Department of Housing and Urban Development; (4) U.S. Department of the Navy (two lists); (5) U.S. Department of the Army; and (6) American Telephone & Telegraph Company.

Overseas Private Investment Corporation (OPIC) Management Competencies*

Technical Knowledge and Skill

(To be stated by each employee.)

---

*Overseas Private Investment Corporation, 1129 Twentieth Street NW, Washington, D.C. 20527. Listing developed by J. Bruce Llewellyn, President, and Richard K. Childress, Vice President for Personnel and Administration, in conjunction with consultants Craig E. Schneier and Alice G. Sargent.

Business Relationships

Has an entrepreneurial orientation and takes initiative.

Uses judgment to promote and protect OPIC's interests in transactions with others.

Builds effective relationships with outside organizations.

Anticipates client needs and desires.

Uses tact in all interactions.

Demonstrates positive, helpful attitude toward clients.

Communications

Communicates with subordinates about priorities, performance expectations, and policies.

Is seen by others as approachable and willing to discuss problems, issues, policies, and assignments.

Keeps supervisors apprised of principal activities, problems, and goals.

Is seen as sensitive to the feelings, viewpoints, and problems of others in individual and group settings.

Is persuasive and able to defend own viewpoint in oral or written communications.

Listens effectively.

Prepares written documents that are clear, well organized, complete, and timely.

Speaks with clarity; is concise and factual.

Makes oral comments that are tactful and appropriately timed and that contribute to group effectiveness.

Initiates interactions with others to solicit their viewpoints.

Sense of Priorities

Keeps a balanced perspective on the organization's priorities even under pressure.

Is not controlled or manipulated by situational or short-lived pressures.

Demonstrates flexibility and ability to compromise.

Is sensitive to work and problems of other units.

Personal and Interpersonal Skills

Has emotional resilience; responds effectively to emotional reactions by others.

Is open to new ideas; is willing to experiment with new approaches or methods.

Responds to power situations without blame, recrimination, or oppressive behavior.

Engages in self-starting behaviors.

Realistically assesses own strengths and weaknesses.

Supervisor Skills and Characteristics

Builds open environment for communication with supervisors, peers, and subordinates.

Demonstrates effectiveness at planning, organizing, controlling, and directing others.

Is sensitive, courteous, and tactful to employees.

Successfully delegates division of labor in the unit.

Coaches and teaches job-related skills.

Establishes realistic employee development plans.

Provides frequent and detailed performance feedback.

Leadership

Communicates high standards for self and others.

Takes initiative to identify and solve potential problems.

Uses authority of own position judiciously to achieve the organization's goals.

Projects positive attitude to staff about the organization's ability to be effective.

Gives clear, complete directions.

Management Team Effectiveness

Builds colleagueships and alliances.

Has compliance-producing skills.

Imparts team spirit and cohesiveness.

Is sensitive to what others are thinking and feeling.

Structures effective meetings.
Balances individual and group needs.

Pedler, Burgoyne, and Boydell
Management Competencies*

Mike Pedler, John Burgoyne, and Tom Boydell selected as "successful managers" (1) executives; (2) up-and-coming managers who were significantly younger than average for their level; and (3) managers of any level and age who were identified as above average in effectiveness. From that population they developed a competency list as follows:

Basic Knowledge and Information

1. *Command of basic facts*—such as goals and plans (long and short term), policies, who's who in the organization, roles and relationships between various departments, and one's own job and what is expected.

2. *Relevant professional knowledge*—technical knowledge, such as production technology, marketing techniques, engineering knowledge, relevant legislation, sources of finance, and knowledge of basic management principles and theories.

Skills

1. *Continuing sensitivity to events*—is open to "hard" information (figures and facts) and "soft" information (feelings of other people).

2. *Analytical, problem-solving, and decision-making skills*—uses logical, optimizing techniques; is able to weigh pros and cons in what is basically a very uncertain or ambiguous situation, calling for a high level of judgment or even intuition.

3. *Social skills and abilities*—has skills in communicating, delegating, negotiating, resolving conflict, persuading, selling, and using and responding to authority and power.

*Copyright © 1978 McGraw-Hill Book Company (UK) Limited. From Mike Pedler, John Burgoyne, and Tom Boydell, *A Manager's Guide to Self-Development*. Used by permission.

Personal Qualities

1. *Emotional resilience*—feels the stress but is able to cope with it by maintaining self-control and by giving to some extent.

2. *Proactivity: inclination to respond purposefully to events*—relates immediate responses to longer-term goals; sees a job through; is dedicated and committed; has a sense of mission; takes responsibility for things that happen rather than passing the buck to someone else.

3. *Creativity*—is able to come up with unique responses to situations; has the insight to recognize and take up useful new approaches.

4. *Mental agility*—is able to think of several things at once, switch rapidly from one problem or situation to another, and grasp the whole situation or problem quickly (rather than ponderously ploughing through all components).

5. *Balanced learning habits and skills*—is an independent learner; takes responsibility for the "rightness" of what is learned rather than depending passively and uncritically on an authority; is capable of abstract thinking as well as concrete, practical thought; is able to use a range of learning processes, such as discovery and reflection.

6. *Self-knowledge*—is aware of role, goals, values, and feelings.

U.S. Department of Housing and Urban Development Factors for Candidate Development*

Leadership: Ability to take charge; to direct, motivate, develop, and coordinate the activities of others; to achieve results through effective delegation to the appropriate person(s); to provide guidance, follow-up, and control.

Oral communication: Ability to present oral information effectively and clearly; to persuade or influence others through oral presentation.

---

*Assessors at the U.S. Department of Housing and Urban Development use this list of factors for its candidate development program. For further information, contact Ronald O. Hietala, Staff Psychologist, HUD, 451 Seventh Street SW, Washington, D.C. 20410.

Interpersonal skill: Ability to be sensitive and to perceive the needs, feelings, and capabilities of others; to deal effectively with others regardless of status or position; to accept interpersonal differences and develop rapport with others.

Perception: Ability to identify, assimilate, and comprehend the critical elements of a situation; to evaluate factors essential to the solution of a problem; to understand people and what they *really* say.

Decisiveness: Ability to make decisions, render judgments, take action, make commitments, and not change decisions when challenged; to take initiative in acting when required.

Organizing and planning: Ability to establish courses of action for self and/or others to attain specific results; to make effective use of personnel and other resources; to establish objectives, schedules, and priorities.

Judgment: Ability to apply logical and sound judgment in use of resources; to determine and generate courses of action; to define solutions to problems in the context of social and organizational attitudes.

Written communication: Ability to present information effectively and clearly in writing; to persuade and influence others through written presentation.

Adaptability: Ability to modify behavior and approaches in dealing with different situations.

Stress management: Ability to maintain an effective task-oriented level of behavior in light of circumstances such as time constraints, differing attitudes of others, lack of pertinent information, and limitation of resources and/or personnel.

U.S. Department of the Navy
Cross-Validated Competencies*

Concern for Efficiency and Effectiveness

Sets goals and performance standards
Takes initiative

Management Control

Plans and organizes
Optimizes use of resources
Delegates
Monitors results
Rewards
Disciplines

Skillful Use of Influence

Influences
Team-builds
Develops subordinates (coaches)
Shows self-control

Advising and Counseling

Has positive expectations
Has realistic expectations
Understands

Conceptual Thinking

Conceptualizes
Applies concepts to a job situation

*U.S. Department of the Navy, "Cross-Validated Competencies, as Clustered and Labeled for Instructional Purposes in the Navy Leadership and Management Education Training (LMET) Program" (1980).

U.S. Department of the Navy

| DEVELOPING OBJECTIVES | GETTING COMMITMENT TO OBJECTIVES |

DEVELOPING OBJECTIVES

Establishing Standards

Establishing challenging objectives with the people who report to you.

Demonstrating strong professional commitment to, and persistence in, achieving your unit's or work group's mission.

Communicating high professional standards formally and informally.

Creating Clarity

Establishing clear, specific objectives and standards for the jobs of people who report to you.

Helping the people who report to you to understand how their jobs contribute to the overall mission of their unit or work group.

Making sure the role each person will play in accomplishing a task is clear.

GETTING COMMITMENT TO OBJECTIVES

Mutuality

Giving the people who report to you a chance to influence the objectives and standards that are set for their jobs.

Asking the people who report to you to participate in setting deadlines for the achievement of their objectives.

Asking people who report to you to participate in deciding on the priorities of their jobs.

Support

Paying close attention to what the people who report to you are saying when they talk with you.

When making assignments, trying to make the best use of strengths and abilities of the people who report to you.

Building helpful, positive relationships with the people in your unit or work group.

Management Practices

COACHING TO ACHIEVE TARGET PERFORMANCE

Communicating

Explaining the cause of problems so that those who report to you can correct them.

Encouraging the people who report to you to be open in telling you about their mistakes.

Expecting the people who report to you to find and correct errors and problems on their own.

Periodically trying to get a feel for the morale of your unit or work group.

Helping and Rewarding

Using recognition, praise and other nonmonetary rewards for top performance.

Helping the people who report to you get the cooperation of other departments.

Giving clear-cut decisions to the people who report to you when they need them.

APPRAISING PERFORMANCE

Providing Feedback

Giving feedback to the people who report to you on how they are doing in their jobs.

Being willing to revise plans and objectives when circumstances warrant the change.

Recognizing the people who report to you for good performance more than criticizing them for performance problems.

Communicating your views honestly and directly during discussions of the performance of those who report to you.

Conducting Appraisals

Using performance appraisals to help people who report to you improve their future performance.

Working with the people who report to you reach mutual agreement on their performance appraisals.

U.S. Department of the Army Leadership Profiles*

Profile Of The Successful Military Leader (GO)
At Senior Executive Levels

Strong self-image

Self-starter

Strong success orientation

- Deals with complex problems by conceptualizing in terms of total systems, subsystems, and processes
- Aggressive in dealings outside the organization
- Takes initiative in determining strategies for formulating goals and articulating policy
- Influences others with an interpersonal style that is confidently assertive but less dramatic and spectacular
- Highly situational and less coercive with subordinates, delegates real responsibility and accountability
- Activity not limited to areas of proven expertise and high confidence
- Concern with subordinates is concentrated primarily on their support and development
- Sees own self-development as an on-going process of self-assessment and self-management; seeks developmental opportunities outside as well as within the institution.

Profile Of The Successful Military Leader (COL)
At Senior Management Levels

Strong self-image

Self-starter

Strong success orientation

- Deals with complex problems by conceptualizing in terms of problem elements, functions, and tasks
- Aggressive with peers and subordinates
- Takes initiative in determining strategies for accomplishing goals and implementing policy
- Influences others with an interpersonal style that is charismatic and highly visible
- Highly active and directive with subordinates; delegates hesitantly
- Tends to focus activity in areas of proven expertise and high confidence
- Concern with subordinates is concentrated primarily on their supervision and performance evaluation.
- Sees own self-development as a product of past experiences and opportunities provided by the institution

---

TRANSITION INVOLVES CHANGES IN (1) interpersonal relationships, (2) group and organizational dynamics, (3) information processing and decision making, and (4) self-management

---

*From Bradford F. Spencer and Jerald R. Gregg, "Successful Behaviors Which Breed Failure," *University of Michigan Business Review* (1979). Developed by John Hallen, consultant, Washington, D.C., and Lt. Col. Frank L. Burns, U.S. Army.

American Telephone & Telegraph Company
Management Assessment Center Dimensions*

Administrative Skills

Organizing and planning
Decisiveness
Decision quality

Interpersonal Skills

Leadership skills
Oral communication skills
Forcefulness
Awareness of social environment
Behavior flexibility

Stability of Performance

Tolerance of uncertainty
Resistance to stress

Intellectual Ability

General mental ability

Written communication skills

Work-oriented Motivation

Inner work standards
Energy
Self-objectivity

Career Orientation

Need advancement

Independence

Independence of others

I have integrated a list of competencies from the various models and described them as masculine, neutral, or feminine as follows:

Masculine	*Neutral*	*Feminine*
Analytical problem-solving and decision-making skills	Relevant professional knowledge	Self-knowledge
	Continuing sensitivity to events	Emotional resilience
Proactivity—inclination to respond purposefully to events	Mental agility	Creativity
	Balanced learning habits and skills	Social skills and abilities

It is obvious that the masculine qualities are valued more highly in the workplace, but that many of the feminine qualities are relevant for management in the 1980s.

*Sample provided by American Telephone & Telegraph Company, showing the management assessment dimensions used in one of its assessment programs. Further information can be obtained from Douglas W. Bray, AT&T, 1776 On-the-Green, Room 48-2B48, Morristown, N.J. 07960.

Appendix C
Self-Assessment Instruments for Masculine and Feminine Behaviors

Androgyny Scales

There are two androgyny scales: (1) the Bem Sex-Role Inventory (see Appendix A), developed by Sandra Bem, previously at Stanford University and now in the Psychology Department at Cornell University,[1] and (2) the Spence, Helmreich & Stapp Personal Attributes Questionnaire, developed at the University of Texas.[2] Both are based on the notion that people do not have to give up their current masculine or feminine behavior, but instead can add to their present repertoires.

FIRO B: Fundamental Interpersonal Relationship Orientation Behavior

The dimensions of the FIRO B scale, developed by William Schutz, are the interpersonal needs of inclusion, control, and affection.[3] The scale is both input and output model, assessing to what extent the person expresses and to what extent the person wishes for this kind of behavior. In my experience, many women begin work with high expressed inclusion and affection, and low expressed control. After their organizational socialization takes place, however, the expressed control increases and the expressed inclusion and affection decreases. This very much parallels what Rosabeth Moss Kanter says are the pitfalls of being relegated to the helper, mother, nurturant role.[4] Colleagues tend to bring their personal problems to the woman, but they do not ask her advice on organizational problems. Her nurturant behavior limits her role to mothering, and her affectionate behavior limits her to being a sex object. A number of women eventually suppress their tenderness and become the stoical iron maidens.

In their study of 25 highly successful women managers, Margaret Hennig and Anne Jardim discovered that the managers found their jobs easier if they did not get involved in personal relationships at work. At age 40, however, such "Queen Bee" women tended to question the costs of that choice.[5] The reaction of black women is even more drastic. It is still not surprising to hear black women say that they have adapted to rejection by denying their own needs for inclusion. The decision is to adopt an exclusively high task/low relationship style.

It is essential for a woman to increase her expressed control within several years of entry, since that's what is rewarded in the marketplace. Either the Strength Deployment Inventory or the Myers-Briggs Inventory might be used instead of (or in addition to) FIRO to measure expressed control.

Management of Differences (MODE): Thomas-Kilman

The MODE inventory, developed by Kenneth Thomas and Ralph Kilman,[6] describes five styles for dealing with differences: collaboration, competition, compromise, accommodation, and avoidance. The dimensions are categorized as assertiveness (masculine) and cooperativeness (feminine). It is not unusual for high-level managers to score high on competition and zero on accommodation. Their attitude is: "Why accommodate? You go in and fight it out, and if you lose you go on to the next battle. Why should I have to help you get your needs met and be so concerned with participation? If you can't do it for yourself, you don't belong here."

Influence Scales

David Berlew and Roger Harrison developed influence scales that assess (1) participation and trust; (2) assertive persuasion (a rational, logical thinking style); (3) common vision; and (4) reward and punishment (coercive power).[7] Berlew and William LeClere, in a subsequent modification of this instrument, added a fifth scale: disengaging, or a tactical withdrawal from influence situations. Kenneth Blanchard and Paul Hersey developed the Power Perception Profile, which utilizes seven bases of power: coercive, connection, expert, information, legitimate or position, referent, and reward.[8]

Another useful assessment instrument is the Blanchard-Hersey Lead Self, which looks at high task/high relationship, high task/low relationship, low task/high relationship, and low relationship/low task styles. Women tend toward a high relationship/low task or high relationship/high task style. Usually, it is critical for women to learn a high task/low relationship style if they are to broaden the range of their skills. For many men it is the opposite: in order to have a more complete repertoire, they need to develop a high relationship/high task and high relationship/low task style.[9]

Scales to Assess Managerial Style and Personal Style

The Strength Deployment Inventory, developed by Elias Porter,[10] has three basic motivation patterns: (1) altruistic—nurturing and promoting harmony among others (primarily a feminine style); (2) assertive—enjoying directing the patterns of others (a masculine style); and (3) analytical—achieving self-sufficiency, self-reliance, and logical orderliness (again, a more masculine style).

The Myers-Briggs Type Indicator[11] is a rich assessment instrument that has the following typology:

Extrovert — Introvert
Sensing — Intuitive
Thinking — Feeling
Judging — Perceptive

The more feminine behaviors are intuitive, feeling, and perceptive. The more masculine behaviors are sensing, thinking, and judging.

NOTES

1. Sandra Bem, "Psychological Androgyny," in Alice G. Sargent, ed., *Beyond Sex Roles* (St. Paul: West Publishing Co., 1977), pp. 319–325.
2. Janet T. Spence and Robert L. Helmreich, *Masculinity and Femininity: Their Psychological Dimensions, Correlates, and Antecedents* (Austin: University of Texas Press, 1978).
3. William C. Schutz, *FIRO: A Three-Dimensional Theory of Interpersonal Behavior* (New York: Rinehart, 1958).
4. Rosabeth Moss Kanter, *Men and Women of the Corporation* (New York: Basic Books, 1977).
5. Margaret Hennig and Anne Jardim, *The Managerial Woman* (New York: Doubleday, 1977).
6. Kenneth W. Thomas and Ralph H. Kilman, "Management of Differences Inventory," School of Business, University of California, Los Angeles, 1972.
7. "Positive Power and Influence Program." Published by Situation Management Systems, Inc., Box 476, Center Station, Plymouth, Mass. 02361.
8. Paul Hersey and Kenneth H. Blanchard, "Blanchard-Hersey Power Perception Profile," 1979. Available from University Associates & Learning Resources Corp., 8517 Production Road, San Diego, Cal. 92121.
9. Paul Hersey and Kenneth H. Blanchard, "Lead Self," 1973. Available from University Associates & Learning Resources Corp.

10. "Strength Deployment Inventory." Published by Personal Strength
    Assessment Service, Inc., P.O. Box 397, Pacific Palisades, Cal. 90272.
11. "Myers-Briggs Type Indicator." Available from the Center for Appli-
    cations of Psychological Type, P.O. Box 13807, University Station,
    Gainesville, Fla. 32604.

Index

vicarious achievement ethnic, 46

Weaver, Earl, 97–98
women
  abdication of control by, 25
  adult development of, 156–157
  androgynous behavior of, at
    home, 182–183
  autonomy and, 158
  entrance of, into work environ-
    ment, 15
  in groups, 60–62
  as managers, see women managers
  masculine behavior of, 5
  as minority, 116
  networking among, 11, 74, 160
  stereotyping of, 160
women managers
  aggression, verbal, of, 29
  androgynous, 55–57
  anger in, 27–28
  behavior goals of, 191
  black, 167, 225
  caricature of, 10
  competence of, 21–23, 166–167
  control and, 25–26
  dependency as issue for, 31–35
  development of androgynous be-
    havior in, 72–74
  emotional expression by, 22,
    26–29
  in groups, 130
  humiliation of, 33
  intimidation of, 33
  lack of confidence in, 56
  masculine traits necessary for, 56
  networks and, 74
  in parent-child relationships,
    31–35

problems facing, 165–168
recognizing stereotypical behavior in, 69–70
relationships of, with male managers, 168–171, 178–179
relationships of, with women, 74
resistance of, to masculine style, 4
sexual issues and, 175
stress and, 146–147
suppression of feminine characteristics in, 57
susceptibility of, to competitive
  style, 9
training for, 74
transaction orientation of, 27
traveling as sexual issue for, 176–
  179
Type A behavior in, 142
women's liberation movement, 6–7
Woolf, Virginia, 3
work as self-fulfillment, 156
worker rap groups, 77
working parents
  family responsibilities of, 11–12
  public policy supporting, 185–
    187
work relationships
  barriers in, 16
  intensity of, 120
  inventory of, 110–113
  male-female, see male-female rela-
    tionships
  rating, 122–130
work schedules, alternative, 186

Xerox Corporation, 80, 150

Yankelovich, Daniel, 76–77, 78
Young, Lewis, 60

The Androgynous Manager

ALICE G. SARGENT

Androgyny, which is a blend of the characteristics of both sexes, is a word you will be
hearing more and more in our rapidly evolving
society. "Androgynous manager" is a term that
Alice Sargent has coined to define her concept
of what it will take to be an effective leader in
the 1980s. The androgynous manager will
blend personality traits that custom has prescribed as properly "belonging" only to one
sex or the other.

But custom, like anything else, can be wrong.
If managers are to survive in this age of changing expectations among the workforce, they
will need to cultivate both compassion and
assertiveness, both sympathy and toughmin-
dedness. Daily work situations demand no
less. Does it really contribute to getting the
work done to come on like a chaingang boss to
someone who wants time off to take care of a
personal problem? Or to shrink from the loud-
mouth who insists that there is only one way to
do something?

No, says Alice Sargent. Such daily situations
call for a blend of traditionally feminine and
masculine traits. And there is no reason why
any manager cannot learn to respond with an
androgynous blend of feeling and action. To
assume otherwise is to fall victim to prejudice,
bias, or superstition, and no modern manager
can afford to do so.

What are the characteristics of the androgynous manager? More important, what are
the benefits of androgynous behavior to the